A Rainbow Book

To James
With love from
Grandfather

The
Choices
Are
Yours

*How
Values-Driven Choices
Change Lives*

Distributor 1-800-356-9315

ROBERT J. TURLEY

Rainbow Books, Inc.
FLORIDA

Library of Congress Cataloging-In-Publication Data

Turley, Robert J.
    The choices are yours : how values-driven choices change
lives / Robert J. Turley.
        p.   cm.
    Includes bibliographical references.
    ISBN 1-56825-062-2 (acid-free paper)
    1. Christian ethics. I. Title.
BJ1261.T87 1997
241--dc21   97-14155
                                                                    CIP

The Choices Are Yours:
How Values-Driven Choices Change Lives
Copyright 1998 © Robert J. Turley

Published by Rainbow Books, Inc.
P. O. Box 430
Highland City, FL 33846-0430 USA
Editorial Offices Telephone/Fax (941) 648-4420
Email: NAIP@aol.com
Individual Orders: Telephone (800) 356-9315, Fax (800) 242-0036

Several brief quotes have been reprinted by permission, as follows:
There's No Such Thing as a Free Lunch by Milton Friedman, published by Open Court Trade & Academic Books (Copyright © 1975);
and *The Closing of the American Mind* by Allan Bloom, published by
Simon & Schuster (Copyright © 1987).

Cover and interior design by Betsy A. Lampé

Manufactured in the United States of America.

This book is dedicated to the glory of God, and to young people who need to know that their lives will be fashioned by their choices.

Contents

Acknowledgments

John Donne taught us that "no man is an island." None of us can do anything worthwhile without the help of others. If this book is worthless, the blame is mine. But, if it is at all useful, I must acknowledge the great help of these others and express to them my gratitude.

My parents and our extended family never wavered in their insistence that we children know right from wrong and do right. My teachers, at school and Sunday school, taught the same values. I grew up in a small town, where it seemed to us that all adults required good behavior; and none looked the other way when we were tempted to misbehave. My memories are of the culture about which I have written; and I well realize that I was blessed by the willingness of previous generations to pass that culture on to mine.

My four wonderful children, Leighton Isaacs, Lynn McComas, Joe Turley, and Mavis Scully, throughout their lives have been a constant challenge to thoughtfully answer: "Why, Daddy? Why?" They helped to teach me lessons which

I hope this book passes on to others, including my eight grandchildren. They also helped select the suggested reading list. My extraordinary friend, Susan Graves Tebbs, was a source of remarkable encouragement throughout the many times she patiently listened to all of my problems in writing this book and getting it published. My secretary, Pamela Gieringer, has conquered the daunting task of reading my handwriting and interlineations so that we could work through draft after redraft after redraft until we got the manuscript ready for the publisher. Betty Wright and Betsy Lampé have guided me through the strange world of book publishing, and they have edited my work with great care. My profound thanks to all of them. Without their help, this book would not be the same; perhaps not even done.

Lexington, Kentucky
April, 1997

Introduction

This is a book about your life. Not about what has happened so far, but about how your future will depend upon you and your choices. This is a book about choices, and how to make them. Like it or not, you must make choices; and those choices will have consequences for which you will be responsible and which will help to shape your life. In the preface to *The Great Divorce*, C. S. Lewis wrote:

> ... We are not living in a world where all roads are radii of a circle and where all, if followed long enough, will therefore draw gradually nearer and finally meet at the centre: rather in a world where every road, after a few miles, forks into two, and each of those into two again, and at each fork you must make a decision.[1]

---

[1] C. S. Lewis, *The Great Divorce* (New York: Macmillan, 1946), pp. 5-6.

There is no escape from choices. Neither is there escape from the consequences of those choices, for which you are accountable. So your choices must be made in accord with internalized values about which you will read here; or else your choices will bring misery to you, to those around you, and to those affected by your choices. In this book I'll tell you how to make wise choices, with good consequences.

A lot of life is related to words, because one of the ways in which people communicate with each other is by using words. Our ideas are formed and then expressed by words. Love is expressed by words. Sometimes fights are started with words. Too often misunderstanding is generated by words. Usually this is because the speaker and his listener, or the writer and his reader don't give the same meaning to the words. Books are words on paper. To reduce the chances of misunderstanding this message I have written for you, I will explain what I mean by some of the important words, especially the abstract words. Some I will explain in the text, and others in the "Glossary" at the end of the book. I agree with Pope John Paul II, who said: "My explanation begins by clarifying words and concepts." [2]

Some folks may have to use a dictionary to understand some of the words I use, but that's good. It will increase your vocabulary and help develop your communication skills. I shall make no apology for causing you to develop your skills. On the contrary, I will try to help you do so.

Hopefully, this book will be one of many sources from which you can learn good things. But learning those things is not the end. You must internalize them. That means you must make the good things you learn a part of you and your own thought processes. For example, when you learn the Golden Rule, you should internalize its principle so that,

---

[2] John Paul II, *Crossing the Threshold of Hope* (New York: Alfred A. Knopf, 1994), p. 4.

even without thinking, you treat other people in the way you would like to be treated.

This book speaks candidly about a relationship with God. That really wasn't my intention when I began to write it. I was going to write about life and how to live it with an internalized set of moral and ethical standards. As I wrote, I found that my thoughts about morals and ethics cannot be expressed without reference to the Judeo-Christian heritage of which we are heirs.

This book is Christian. I make no apology for that. Even so, I'm inclined to be inclusionary rather than exclusionary when I think of the Creator and His infinite grace. Jews, Christians and Muslims all worship the same God; and we share with each other the whole of the Torah, as well as many other books of the Old Testament. Speaking to some of the Pharisees and describing Himself as the Good Shepherd, Jesus said, "other sheep I have, which are not of this fold: them also I must bring, and they shall hear my voice."[3] So I cannot say that God has made no provision for others, even if I cannot explain what it is.

While speaking of faith, this book is not meant to be a theology textbook. I'm not trained in theology. Moreover, you will see that I believe simple faith to be the nexus between God and man, regardless of theological niceties which I don't always comprehend. That is to say, if we are "saved by faith,"[4] a lack of understanding doesn't condemn us.

What I tell you in this book is not really new. Playing the role of Solomon, the "Preacher" tells us that "there is no new thing under the sun."[5] Neither is this book the result of some kind of brilliance on my part. Critics will no doubt call

---

[3] John 10: 16. (Unless otherwise noted, all Biblical references are to the King James Version).

[4] Eph. 2: 8-9.

[5] Eccles. 1: 9.

it unsophisticated, and intellectuals will damn it as simplistic. It doesn't try to break new ground so much as to suggest return to some well-traveled paths, which were proven to lead somewhere worth going.

It is not written for the intellectuals. Instead it is directed toward plain people; some of whom haven't matriculated, much less graduated. It proceeds from the belief that what is good and right and true and worthy does not need intellectual endorsement so much as it needs to be passed on from one generation to the next, with some assurance that it is best for the individual and his community. We should feel free to say: "Don't cheat." Not because cheaters never win. Sometimes they do. But you will respect yourself only if you win without cheating.

Finally, this is not just a book of rules which will make life easy for you. Indeed, some things I say will appear to make your life more difficult; because I'll speak of your responsibility for your own life.

Chapter One

From Your Present "You"
To Your Future "Who"

You are unique. There is no one in this world just like you. You are not the same as anybody else. You may look like your father or a sister or even a twin, but you are unique. That means that you are one of a kind.

Oh, you may have a talent for music or sports or reading comprehension like many other people, but they're not really the same. No one else has exactly the same mixture of talents that you have. Neither does anybody else have the same environment that you have. Even though there are likenesses, there are also dissimilarities. We all share some traits which we sometimes call "human nature," but we are all nevertheless quite different from each other.

So you must be very careful as to how, if ever, you compare yourself to other people.

To compare scores in golf or tennis or to compare techniques in diving, dance or public speaking is commonplace. In areas such as those, we not only compare our results with those of others, we compare the results of our efforts with results which we, ourselves, have had at other times. Such comparisons can show us whether we are improving as we train ourselves to do better and better. But these things which can be quantified or measured or assessed are not of themselves the measure of a person. If you score better on Friday than you did on Tuesday, you are not necessarily a better person for having done so. Neither are you less worthy on Friday than on Tuesday if your score is not so good. Certainly, if you beat someone else at tennis, you are not a better person than your opponent, you have only played better at a particular time and place.

There is only one comparison of personal worth that can be legitimately made: To compare yourself to your own potential. If you have done the best you can do, you are to be commended even if someone else has won the race or if you have had a better score on another occasion. But if you don't measure up to your own potential, you can fairly be disappointed in yourself and try harder to do better.

One of the saddest things to see is a parent or a teacher who compares a child to a brother or sister. Parents and teachers should know better. Each child should be judged on his or her own potential, not in competition for personal worth with a brother or a sister. Don't compare yourself with others and don't let others compare you with themselves. Don't compare yourself with others and don't let parents or teachers do so. Judge yourself and be judged only by your own potential. Remember you're not equal, you're unique.

Almost everybody dreams about the future. Do you ever wonder who you will become?

The social scientists tell us that we are the products of heredity and environment. They even call it "nature and nurture." While they argue between themselves as to which is more important, they talk only about genes and external influences. I think they overlook a very important factor — choices. You will become the person who is fashioned by your genes, the place and people with whom you live, and your own choices.

Do you look like your mother and some of her family, or like your father and some of his? Do you have a talent for music like your grandmother, or for athletics like your uncle? Do your sisters and brothers have aptitudes and talents like your own, or do they differ from you and from each other?

Through the use of modern technology, cell biologists are now looking inside the cells which make up the tissues of our bodies. Among their discoveries is deoxyribonucleic acid, which is commonly called DNA. They tell us that the DNA that each of us inherits — some elements from father and other elements from mother — is the determinant throughout a lifetime of the replication, growth, longevity and activity of our cells, and thus our physical structure. They also say that the DNA of each person differs from that of everyone else except an identical twin.

The scientific discipline that studies the effects of DNA is called genetics. Geneticists examine questions such as how certain inherited characteristics come about, why the body responds as it does to their influence, and what might be done to intervene in this process so as to enhance the beneficial and suppress the harmful. They say that from the moment of conception, when the genes from each of two parents combine to form the new DNA of their child, the child's individual physical characteristics are influenced from before birth, during life, and even unto death.

So, the person whom you will become is affected by heredity; and, this is especially true of your physical attributes. According to the Bible, "Which of you by taking thought can add one cubit unto his stature?"[6]

This is not an excuse for fatalism or resignation to lack of control over some of the influences on your life. Heredity

---

[6] Matt. 6:27

is not a license to walk away from the challenges of life. On the contrary, it is by way of heredity that God gives you talents to be utilized in serving the purpose for which He has given and preserved your life.

You can't change your heredity; genes are for a lifetime. Because of other people and natural forces, you cannot control your environment. Even if you move someplace else or if you are elected President, there are few things which you yourself can do to change your environment. You can only adapt to it.

On the other hand, you *can* make the choices which will change your life; and only *you* can do so. Other people can influence you, to be sure; but only you can make your choices. Not even God will change your life unless you let Him do so, He has left you free to make your own choices, including even whether you will believe He exists.

Your choices are your own decisions. They may be unimportant, such as which clothes to wear today; or they may be very important, such as your choice of a career or who you marry. Some of your most important choices will be made when you are quite young. The choices of your spouse, your career and your habitat are especially vital to your adult life and must be made at its beginning.

As we've seen, your choices can have a great influence on the person you will become. That means that you must make wise choices or, in other words, good decisions.

Decision-making is an essential part of living. You would think that everybody knows how to make decisions because everybody makes decisions. But, many decisions are unwisely made because few people have good decision-making skills. These skills can be developed; and to your benefit.

There are four essentials to wise decision-making. They include: (1) Information — nobody has a right to be wrong on the facts; (2) Analysis of alternatives — consider and compare the risks and benefits of each; and (3) Timing — choose that alternative with the greater advantages and fewer disadvantages, but don't jump too soon or wait too long.

That all sounds simple, and many people think it is too simple to apply to complex circumstances. Yet even the most complex circumstances can be broken down into separate parts so that decision-making can be simplified. It takes thought, self-discipline and practice; but it can be done.

Fourth, and most important, your decisions must be consistent with a system of values. In spite of the popular catch phrase "equal choice," options are seldom equal. Some are just plain wrong. You should consciously consider whether your choices are morally and ethically right, whether they are fair to other people or simply self-serving, and whether they are consistent with your understanding of God's will and plan for your life. Even if your information, your analysis, and your timing are right, unless your values are a part of your choice, your choice can be wrong and can lead to horrendous consequences.

You must never forget that there are consequences to your choices, for yourself and for others, some intended and some unintended. There are consequences to purposeful actions, to mistakes, to carelessness, to failures to act, and so on. There *are* consequences. Consequences may not be immediate, but consequences there will be. As there is a difference between right and wrong, so there is a difference between their consequences. This means that one must think beforehand. One must ask himself, "What will be the consequences? Will they be good? Will somebody be helped? Will somebody be hurt? What will be the consequences of this action?"

I must caution you here that, in the same way that you bear responsibility for your choices, so likewise do you bear the responsibility for their consequences.

A popular satirist, P. J. O'Rourke, tells a story about his friend's son who was arrested for selling drugs. The author and his friend talk about alternatives to punishment.

Then O'Rourke continues his satirical story, speaking with
heavy sarcasm:

> . . . And it wasn't until I'd hung up that I realized
> what we'd been saying. My friend's kid didn't need
> to suffer any consequences, not serious conse-
> quences, anyway. After all, addiction is a sickness
> and he needs treatment. Besides, he's got personal
> problems and comes from a broken home. It's not
> like he's a criminal or anything. If he were a crimi-
> nal, he'd be poorer and darker skinned.
>
> My friend's kid lives in a well-padded little uni-
> verse, a world with no sharp edges or hard sur-
> faces. It's the Whiffle Ball again. The kid leads a
> Whiffle Life, and so does my friend and so do I
>
> We're Americans. These are modern times.
> Nothing bad is going to happen to us. If we get
> fired, it's not failure; it's a mid-life vocational reas-
> sessment. If we screw up a marriage, we can get
> another one. There's no shame in divorce. Day care
> will take the kids, and the ex-wife can go back to
> the career she was bitching about leaving. If we
> get convicted of a crime, we'll go to tennis prison
> and probably not even that. We'll just have to futz
> around doing community service for a while. Or
> maybe we can tearfully confess everything, join a
> support group and get off the hook by listening to
> shrinks tell us we don't like ourselves enough. Hell,
> play our cards rights, and we can get a book con-
> tract out of it. We don't have to be serious about
> the drug problem — or anything else.[7]

---

[7] P. J. O'Rourke, *Parliament of Whores* (New York: Morgan Entrekin,
The Atlantic Monthly Press, 1991), p. 121.

And so it is when the psychologists and social scientists convince us that we are all victims who bear no personal responsibility for our actions or their consequences. It's always somebody else's fault. There is no sense of responsibility in a counterculture geared to "self-esteem." Psychology, once the study of human behavior, has turned into an exercise in finding excuses for misbehavior. The euphemisms are "alternative lifestyle" or "residual of childhood abuse" or "lack of self-esteem." Anything but responsibility.

But they are dead wrong. The freedom to make choices carries with it the responsibility for those choices. To play the victim or to blame somebody else is unworthy of anyone who wants to be free to make his own choices.

Individual responsibility is the very foundation of freedom. Anything else is anarchy. Self-centeredness may be normal, but a community cannot exist where everybody is self-centered. Everybody must bear responsibility for the spirit of community. The development of civilization has been the definition and redefinition of the relationship between the individual and his community. A balance must be found between rights and responsibilities. Equilibrium comes only when an individual enjoys limited freedom; when his freedom benefits the community, and is not destructive of the fabric or the cohesiveness of the community. So you see, the failure to take responsibility is, in and of itself, destructive of the community, regressive with respect to civilization.

Everybody wants to take the credit, but nobody wants to take the blame. Ask yourself the questions: "What do I deserve? What have I earned? Is it credit or is it blame?" You will make some mistakes. Everybody does. Some things won't turn out like you expect them to because circumstances will change or something wholly beyond your control will happen. Don't despair. Accept responsibility, but pick yourself up and start over. If you need forgiveness, ask for it; but don't dodge the responsibility for your choices and their consequences.

Likewise, the "free will" by which you can accept or reject God's purpose for your life carries responsibility. It's your choice. You are free to choose. If you reject Him or ignore His claim on your life, you will live with the consequences, — like them or not. Don't blame God, — or "fate", — or your parents, — and try to escape responsibility. There is a consistent theme which runs throughout the Old and New Testaments, calling for repentance. In simple terms, repentance means that one must accept responsibility and turn away from the wrong choices.

Chapter Two

What Are "Values"?

*T*hroughout this book you will find references to "values" or a "system of values." In the sense in which "values" is being used, it means principles, standards, or qualities which are considered to be worthwhile or desirable. A system of values, then, consists of multiple values the relative importance of which is recognized by a person or group. Values and systems of values are related to the cultures which accept them; and different cultures accept different systems of values. So we come to speak of "cultural values" as those which are recognized by and acceptable to a people who are, at least in part, held together by the commonality of their values.

You have no doubt recognized that there are also subcultures, which share some values with the predominant group, but which have a supplemental system of values which they apply only to themselves.

It is through a system of values that choices are made. Its system of values is the yardstick by which a culture mea-

sures what is right and what is wrong, what is good and
what is better, and what is bad and what is worse. This
means that those people who share a culture believe their
values to be worthwhile, which is to say worth the cost in
terms of price, sacrifice, loss or penalty incurred as a consequence of choices made in accordance with their values.
      James L. Dennis, a Justice of the Louisiana Supreme
Court, said it this way:

> . . . An ethic is a whole system of moral values that
> individuals or groups follow in deciding how they
> ought to live, what their responsibilities are, and
> what they ought to teach the next generation. Ra-
> tional people hardly ever live without an ethic or a
> system of moral values, and they usually inherit
> their values from previous generations. . . .[8]

Commenting on a book by Robert Bellah and others,[9]
Dennis went on to write:

> Bellah and his associates conclude that over the
> past century the American mind has been captured
> by a single ethic or tradition: an extreme form of
> utilitarian individualism, an uncontrolled pursuit
> of material wealth. They contend that this indi-
> vidualism is overshadowing our other important
> ethical traditions — the biblical and republican tra-
> ditions — and that it may be threatening the sur-
> vival of freedom by isolating Americans from one
> another and undermining the conditions of freedom.

---

[8] James L. Dennis, "For the Common Good," *Trial* (September 1990), p.
      56.
[9] Robert Bellah, et al., *Habits of the Heart: Individualism and Commit-
      ment in American Life* (1985).

He concluded his paper by saying:

> ... Our ethical problems today are not susceptible to merely political solutions. They are moral defects calling for a re-discovery of fundamental principles and a determination to put these principles into practice. . . .[10]

A satirical examination of "what makes people good" was written by David Martin, Emeritus Professor of Sociology at the London School of Economics. After making the point that almost everybody agrees that people should be good but nobody offers an appropriate remedy for the lack of goodness among people, Martin writes:

> The other notion blocking proposals to help make people good is a secular version of Christianity. It takes off in a thoroughly amiable fashion from an attempt to reverse the balance of denunciation in favor of the victims of history and society. As a result you are not "saved" and "justified" *by* a Victim, as in orthodox Christianity, but by *being* yourself a victim.
> Victimage opens up an unlimited credit line absolving you of all responsibility for the past and for the future. Indeed, in some versions this theology holds that the *only* responsible and guilty people are the rulers of the present American empire or the descendants of the British ex-empire. It follows that you can express a moral opinion only provided you first certify your status as a qualified victim or bow before all approved victims in silent humility.[11]

---

[10] Dennis, *Trial* article, p. 62.
[11] David Martin, "What Makes People Good?" *National Review*, (September 9, 1991), p. 26.

Professor Martin speaks of the irony in characterizing everybody as a victim and thereby avoiding the need for a system of values.

Former Attorney General Elliot Richardson suggests that there are no community values because there is no community. At an American Bar Association meeting more than twenty years ago, he said:

> The problem is that the forces underlying Watergate morality persist. And very importantly among those forces — although not sufficiently appreciated as such — is the decline of a sense of community. A community is a transmitter and sustainer of values. The weakening of a sense of community must inevitably lead to a weakening of values.[12]

General Richardson called for a rebuilding of the necessary interrelationship between rights and obligations.

Values are either derived from experience[13] or delivered by an authoritative source. In either case they must be understood in terms of their purpose. This requires that they be carefully and clearly stated. They must be defined in such a way as to be correctly understood. Otherwise, as they are applied in differing circumstances, they can produce the wrong results. Clearly, application of the "letter of the law" can produce injustice if the "spirit of the law" is misunderstood, forgotten or ignored.

For example, some people are inclined to soften their concepts of some values by the use of softer words than those used by others. They use euphemisms. A euphemism is an

---

[12] *ABA News* (September 1974), p. 3.
[13] See: Oliver Wendell Holmes, Jr., *The Common Law* (Boston: Little, Brown & Co., 1881) p. 1, where it is said: "The life of the law has not been logic: it has been experience."

inoffensive word or a soft word which is substituted for a word which might be offensive or distasteful. Those who would find it clearly wrong to "murder an unborn baby" are far less likely to be critical if they are persuaded that abortion is nothing more than the exercise of "a woman's right to choice," and a "private matter" at that. Those who can state an issue in words of their own choosing can often win the argument by using euphemisms. This is what Stuart Chase has called "the tyranny of words,"[14] and it bears directly upon cultural values.

The definition of values has been a task of priests and lawyers throughout history. Both callings know the difficulty but essentiality of that task, especially in view of the development of varying cultures and changing circumstances. Because I have been a lawyer for nearly 50 years, I have less reluctance than some to deal with this subject.

As we shall later see, values are expressed in morals, ethics and law. In whichever of those contexts, they are meant to benefit the community or its members or both. Indeed, they benefit the community when they prescribe the relative rights of individuals in such terms as to permit peaceful coexistence.

So distinctions must be seen and made between standards which are for the benefit of individuals and those which are for the welfare of the community as a whole. It is only when their purposes are understood that conflicts may be appropriately resolved. All of this is directly and inseparably linked to the sources from which our values are drawn; and we will look to that subject a bit later.

---

[14] Stuart Chase, *Tyranny of Words* (Harcourt Brace, 1959).

Chapter Three

Morals, Ethics and The Law

*T*he essential moral question is whether an act is right or wrong. That depends upon the standard by which it is to be measured. Consequently, we sometimes speak of values as standards of moral behavior, which are applicable in all relationships and circumstances to define right and wrong. When these standards are applied in the context of a business or profession, they are commonly called ethics. Finally, a society's *minimum* standards of acceptable behavior, as defined by a legislature or judicial system, we call the law.[15] Not everything legal is likewise moral. Standards of morals and ethics are higher and more exacting than those of law. That is why the professions have ethical standards which require more than the law alone. In short: we must do what the law requires, and we should do what moral and

---

[15] As the text makes clear, moral standards have been called law, especially in the context of religous writings, but the distinction here is important to understanding today's usage.

ethical standards require. Because the law provides only the minimal standards, everyone is required to conform to the law on penalty of fine, imprisonment, or other punishment. Please don't take what I have said to be a negative view of the law. It is not. I have devoted my whole professional career to the law, and I see both its benefits and its shortcomings. Respect for and obedience to the law is a primary responsibility of citizenship; and this is true even when one disagrees with the law. The law is not perfect, and modification by appropriate means and in changing circumstances is the reason provisions for change are made in our very structure of government. But law is the cement which holds a society together, and the lubricant by which its people live together with minimal friction. As an expression of minimal acceptable standards of behavior, law is essential to any group.

There are ways other than punishment to motivate lawful behavior. Those methods are sometimes more closely related to economics than to the criminal law. Government grants of money or other privileges are almost always conditioned upon the recipient's behavior in a specific way. Very often the power of taxation is exercised in such a fashion as to provide deductions or tax credits to only those who follow the behavior pattern required by the taxing authority. Whether it is by a stick or by a carrot, motivation of behavior in an acceptable way is the aim of the law, which sometimes looks to produce results completely unrelated to moral standards, and which at best is related to the minimal of moral standards.

Current usage refers to several occupations as professions. Here I shall refer to the learned professions of the ministry, medicine and law, each of which requires a specialized type of study undertaken only by those who feel called to make that profession their life's work. Of course, the principles apply as well to other professions. For the ministry, licensure is by church rather than government.

For other professions, completion of a postgraduate course in the relevant professional school and passing a proficiency examination are both required for licensure to practice in the field. To government-sponsored agencies or boards is delegated the responsibility of insuring that those licensed meet these minimum standards of competence. Such agencies or boards also promulgate and enforce standards of behavior or "ethics" for the professions.

The ministry, medicine and the law are similar to each other, in that the practitioner often deals with lay people who are frightened and in need because of spiritual, physical or legal problems with which they cannot deal. This results in the creation of relationships with people who become dependent upon the professional. Their dependency is often accompanied by anxiety. So there is born of the dependency relationship a need to protect the layman from any attempt by an unprincipled professional to take advantage of the relationship.

Professionals deal with each other in sometimes very difficult circumstances, so a spirit of collegiality is necessary as well as desirable. They must be able to trust each other. Civility should mark their behavior toward each other. Together, their competence and this spirit of civility, trust and collegiality we sometimes refer to as professionalism.

Professional ethics are the standards of conduct for professionals, with each other and with the people whom they serve. Ethics prohibit dishonesty, of course, but they go further than that. They require affirmative duties of the professional to put the interests of his parishioner, patient or client above his own interests. This will come as no surprise to those who appreciate the professions as being service-oriented; but those who go into a profession for their own benefit can easily run afoul of ethical standards. Members who break the rules of their profession are a small minority; but they are a source of great embarrassment to ministers, doctors and lawyers who give their own best efforts to service and professionalism. For the most part, professionals are ordinary people who take self-sacrifice for granted in meeting their professional responsibilities. Unfortunately, it is the miscreants who make the news and bring their whole profession into disrepute.

Having said that law is the minimal of moral standards or values, and that ethics are those standards applied in the context of the professions, it remains to consider morals themselves.

In our Judeo-Christian heritage, morals are believed to come from God. The children of Israel considered the standards of behavior delivered by God through Moses and the prophets as "the Law." Even what we today think of as moral standards were law to them because for them there was no distinction between "church and state." Speaking of the Mosaic laws, Dr. William M. Taylor wrote:

> . . . in considering these laws, we must not forget that they were designed for a theocracy. God chose the people for his own, and the people chose God as their king . . .
>
> . . . Sin, where God is the king, becomes also crime; and idolatry not only a moral evil, but a civil treason. . . . We make a distinction — and we rightly make it — between that which is sin, as committed against God, and that which is crime, as committed against the community.[16]

Not only the Jews looked to God for their law. It is also said by Cicero concerning the nature of law that:

---

[16] William M. Taylor, *Moses, the Law-Giver* (Grand Rapids, MI, Baker Book House, 1961 reprint), pp. 256-257.

Of all these things about which learned men dispute there is none more important than clearly to understand that we are born for justice, and that right is founded not in opinion but in nature. There is indeed a true law, right reason, agreeing with nature and diffused among all, unchanging, everlasting, which calls to duty by commanding, deters from wrong by forbidding. . . . Nor is it one law at Rome and another at Athens, one law today and another hereafter; but the same law, everlasting and unchangeable, will bind all nations and all times; and there will be one common lord and ruler of all, even God, the framer and proposer of this law.[17]

To some, obedience to the letter of "the Law" became an end in itself. This is why Jesus called the Pharisees hypocrites, saying to them: "you tithe mint and dill and cumin, and have neglected the weightier matters of the law, justice and mercy and faith; these you ought to have done, without neglecting the others."[18] He said that He came to fulfill the Law, and taught that goodness should come from love of others and not simply by obedience to the letter of the Law. The way of life which He shows us is consistent with the Ten Commandments; but it goes further, much further. For example, He taught: do not murder, and don't even lose your temper.[19] He taught: do not commit adultery, and don't even lust after another man's wife.[20]

---

[17] Cicero, *De Legibus*, II, 4, 10, as quoted in Benjamin Fletcher Wright, Jr., *American Interpretations of Natural Law* (New York: Russell and Russell, Inc., 1962), p. 5.
[18] Matt. 23: 23 (RSV).
[19] Matt. 5: 21-22.
[20] Matt. 5: 27-28.

Allan Bloom wrote:

> There is a perennial and unobtrusive view that morality consists in such things as telling the truth, paying one's debts, respecting one's parents and doing no voluntary harm to anyone.[21]

And he thought that to be less than the whole of morality, even though he went on to say:

> Those are all things easy to say and hard to do; they do not attract much attention, and win little honor in the world.[22]

Our task is even more difficult, because we Christians are called to love God and to love one another. We will hoop "the Law" in spirit if we live lives of love.[23] Morals proceed from love of one another; and the values about which I write to you are moral values which must be interpreted in light of love.

----

[21] Allan Bloom, *The Closing of the American Mind* (New York: Simon & Schuster, 1987), p. 325.
[22] Ibid.
[23] Rom. 13: 8, 10.

Chapter Four

Family Values

*M*uch has been said about "family values," and in a recent presidential campaign the term was ill-defined. Indeed, it was twisted to suggest a measure of self-righteousness in those who endorsed it, especially when the term was used in relation to so-called "nontraditional households." Having had its meaning distorted, users of the term were vilified as having no compassion for others; and a vigorous defense was mounted in support of "single mothers," "gay parents," and other households in which there were no married parents.

As we've seen, behavior can be effectively modified or controlled by the use of euphemisms. Ideas are communicated from person to person by words, and different words can imply approval or disapproval to such extent as to influence the listener to reject or accept the ideas themselves.

An example is the word "bastard." It means illegitimate offspring, and it is a pejorative expression. As more and more girls bear children out of wedlock, that word is no longer in common use to describe their children. Instead, those women

who were once said to birth bastards are now referred to as
"single mothers"; and by that term included with widows
and divorced mothers, as if all were alike. By use of the
term "single mothers," they are portrayed as the norm, if
not even an approved example. So it followed that the liberal
media and entertainment industry rose up in arms when then
Vice-President Dan Quayle was critical of the manner in which
a popular television program accepted with no hint of impro-
priety Murphy Brown's baby, sired during a "one-night stand."

But the consequences of bearing an illegitimate child
are plain and prevalent. The television people don't tell us
the truth about the pain and poverty a baby brings to its
teenage "single mother." Her life and the lives of her family
are forever changed for a moment of "making out" with her
irresponsible boyfriend. Of no less importance is the unde-
served psychological impact to the child. Children need a
good male image in the home. Not only do children tend to
copy what they see, they tend to consider their own family
as the norm. So the need for adults, especially parents, to
set good examples. If there is no father in the home, children are likely to accept as normal behavior what they see
on television or in the streets. Children who do not know a
father miss half their heritage and can look to only a mother's
family, without the stability or continuity afforded by generation after generation of whole families. Such an environment
is plainly and grossly unfair to children born out of wedlock.

But the popular counterculture has made it appear that
sex outside of marriage is the thing to do. So it is that the
number of children born to unmarried teenaged mothers in
the United States increased from 200,000 in 1970 to 365,000
in 1992.[24] As a percentage of all births, those to unmarried

---

[24] U. S. Bureau of the Census, *Statistical Abstract of the United States:
1995*, Table No. 94.

mothers increased from 11% in 1970 to 30% in 1992.[25] The scale of increase is shown by Table 1. From 1970 to 1992 illegitimate births to white mothers increased by 313% and, by 1992, nearly 23% of all white babies born in the United States were bastards.[26] In 1992 more than two-thirds of the babies born to black mothers were illegitimate, compared to 38% in 1970.[27]

Table 1 Numbers of Children Born to Unwed Mothers[1]			
Age of Mothers	1970	1992	Increase
Teenagers	200,000	365,000	+83%
Ages 20-29	168,000	669,000	+298%
Age 30 and over	31,000	191,000	+516%

[1] U.S. Census Bureau, *Statistical Abstract: 1995*, Table 94.

Where are the fathers of all these babies? I've spoken only of the women and children, because the statistics concern them; but, where are the men?

The number of unmarried couples living together with one or more children under 15 years of age increased from 196,000 in 1970 to 1,270,000 in 1994.[28] Is there any doubt that family values have changed?

Eighty-five percent of children under 18 years of age in the United States lived with both parents in 1970; but by

---

[25] Ibid.
[26] Ibid.
[27] Ibid.
[28] U. S. Census Bureau, *Statistical Abstract: 1995*, Table No. 60.

1994 only 69% lived with both parents.[29] From 1970 to 1994 the percentage of family groups headed by the mother, and with no father in the home, increased from 12% to 27% of all family groups.[30] The percentage of children living with only their mothers grew from 11% to 23%, and those living with mothers who had never married from 1% to 9%.[31]

Where is the sense of outrage that all these children are growing up without fathers at home? Who are their male role models? Should a matriarchal society be the norm? Ravi Zacharias characterizes this society as one of "consenting adults victimizing unconsenting children."[32]

In virtually every culture and in every generation, the strongest foundation of a community has been the family. Throughout the history of civilization, the standards of both law and morality have required a marriage contract for conjugal relations and have condemned interference by outsiders in the marriage. Divorce has been permitted but, until recently, it was clearly discouraged. Premarital sex and adultery existed but, because they were condemned by the prevailing culture, they were secretive. Then, in the latter half of this century, the "arts" and the media, especially television, used their powerful influence to depict such practices as the norm. The consequent disruption in personal and family relationships is self-evident. It has touched all of us in one way or another. The so-called "nuclear family" is accepted no longer as the rule, and the whole community suffers as a result.

"Family values" begin with the committed monogamous relationship of husband and wife, whether they have children or not. A loving, sharing relationship between a man

---

[29] U. S. Census Bureau, *Statistical Abstract: 1995*, Table No. 79.
[30] U. S. Census Bureau, *Statistical Abstract: 1995*, Table No. 71.
[31] U. S. Census Bureau, *Statistical Abstract: 1995*, Table No. 79.
[32] Ravi Zacharias, *Can Man Live Without God* (Dallas: Word Publishing, 1994), p. 40.

and his wife is among the greatest of blessings, — to themselves, their families, their friends and the whole community. It is sufficiently precious to warrant enormous care and sacrifice to obtain and preserve. Moreover, without such a marriage, the stability essential to the children's upbringing is missing. Preserving a marriage "for the sake of the children" is best for the children, unless the parents' resentment of each other becomes the theme of the household. Constant and pervasive tension between the parents affects the whole family, and children soon learn to manipulate their parents through that means. Often the children themselves become instruments by use of which their parents express hostility or punish each other.

What we often call "family values" include those which relate to the needs of a child which he cannot meet by himself. They also include those values related to the needs of his parents as, later in his life, they rely upon the child psychologically and sometimes financially. Perhaps no less important are relationships with siblings, both in childhood and as adults, as they share love and support for each other.

It seems obvious, of course, that a child needs food and shelter, care and support. Likewise, he needs love. He also needs role models to teach him how to become a "grown-up," to impart to him a sense and system of moral standards, to teach him the meaning of responsibility in his growth to independence, and to nurture the self-confidence which he develops from the achievement of his goals. He needs help to identify the purpose of his life and to prepare for it.

Professor Bloom has well said:

The family requires the most delicate mixture of nature and convention, of human and divine, to subsist and perform its function. Its base is merely bodily reproduction, but its purpose is the formation of civilized human beings. In teaching a language and providing names for all things, it transmits an interpretation of the order of the whole of things. It feeds on books in which the little polity - the family - believes, which tell about right and wrong, good and bad and explain why they are so. The family requires a certain authority and wisdom about the ways of the heavens and of men.[33]

It is likewise evident that, in their later years, some parents and grandparents have difficulty in taking care of themselves and need the support and assistance of their children. Throughout their lives, parents and children find satisfaction in the love they share with each other and the efforts they make to meet each other's needs.

Compare these family values with the hapless condition of an unmarried mother with a child sired by a boyfriend who abandons all responsibility for his own offspring. This is a child condemned to grow up without the healthy influence of a family. Indeed, the child and his mother may be dependent upon her own single mother, or upon the public welfare system, or upon both. This is not said for any reason other than to underline the importance of what I have called "family values" and to show you why the community can rightly condemn behavior which results in the production of illegitimate children who are, by that fact alone, handicapped in whatever efforts they make to develop productive and successful lives.

Of course it is sex which leads to either the happy establishment of a family or sad consequences. And sex begins to make its demands on adolescents who are growing through the most difficult period of their lives.

---

[33] Bloom, *Closing of the American Mind*, p. 57.

The externals like clothes, music and celebrities change from generation to generation, — and even from year to year. But, inside themselves, teenagers are the same. They all feel shy and insecure. They sometimes act stupid in order to cover up their insecurities. Most are too clumsy, and never have enough money for the things they think they need. The girls think they are not pretty enough, and the boys think themselves homely. Boys and girls both fall in love and are rejected. Most think their parents and teachers demand too much of them. There is no more difficult time of life than the teenage years.

The early teenage years are when we reach puberty and the hormones in both boys and girls bring on an awareness of sex. Given teenagers' insecurity, their need to be loved, and their wish to be popular, the arrival of puberty complicates everything. Sex is not new. The present generation may think they have discovered it for themselves, but it was well known long before they were born. Unmarried sex is not new either; but once it was discouraged by the culture, which tried to avoid the unhappy consequences of unmarried sex. Then in the 1960s came the "sexual revolution." Now it seems that television and the movies focus on little other than sex, both in programming and advertising. Pre-married, unmarried, and adulterous sex is the staple of soap operas. Obscenity cases once involved books which seem tame today. Pornography can be found in even the smallest towns, and is now communicated by computer. The coarseness of what was once "barracks language" has become typical of young people's conversation.

The counterculture prevalent today invites everybody to have sex with anybody. Indeed, it virtually demands promiscuity as the passport to popularity. This is true to such extent that people in high places scoff at those who recommend abstinence; and they offer to deal with the problems created through the "sexual revolution" by passing out contraceptives to schoolchildren. This sex-driven culture ignores or glosses over the consequences of promiscuity, among which are:

• Teenage pregnancies,

• Single mothers,

• Widespread venereal diseases,

• Broken hearts,

• Damaged lives, and

• Misery for teenagers and their families.

This is completely apart from the enormous economic costs to provide medical care, counseling, social work and welfare, much of which is borne by the taxpaying public.

The Bible clearly forbids sex between unmarried people. The seventh of the Ten Commandments forbids adultery, which is sex between two people one or both of whom are married to somebody else.[34] Likewise, sex between any two people not married to each other is condemned.[35]

Sex can be beautiful. It can be a rich, fulfilling experience. On the other hand, sex can be a sordid, degrading expression of brutishness. It can be frustrating and cheapening. It can be used to manipulate a partner, or even for gain. To be a beautiful and enriching experience, sex must involve the giving of one's self and the sharing of another. It cannot be demanded or required. Sex on demand is wrong because

---

[34] Exod. 20: 14.
[35] Exod. 22: 16; Deut. 22: 20-30, 21: 17; Prov. 7; Matt. 15: 19-20; Rom. 1: 26-32.

it impairs the human dignity and the personal integrity of another person. It is no better if pleading leads to seduction. Psychological force is no better than physical force. If sex is no more than satisfaction of an urge or appetite, then it is brutish, not beautiful. So, the only beautiful sexual experience is between two people who so love each other that they want to give themselves to each other, — wholly, completely, and without reservation through marriage.

"But, why marriage? The saying of a few words and the exchange of a ring doesn't of itself create love," you may say; and that is true. "But marriage is an undertaking of such far-reaching consequence that one tries desperately to be sure that love is true beforehand, — and why not sex to test it?" you may ask.

First, "love" is an intangible, and we are sometimes mistaken as to its presence. We can mistake pity or sympathy for love; or confuse physical attraction and romantic mood with love. To try out sex because one thinks he or she is "in love" is to step into the dark, and without any possibility of afterwards undoing what has been done. As I have said, sex involves the dignity of one's person and the integrity of one's personality. Once given, a part is gone. Premarital sex robs one of the most precious gift he may give his bride: unimpaired personal integrity.

Second, sex produces babies, — oftentimes unwanted babies. Sex gets girls pregnant. If the girl is married, everything is great and marvelous. Everybody is proud and happy. But if she's not married, the story is quite different. Babies need homes and families and daddies; and homes and families and daddies come with marriage. Any baby born of a premarital sexual relationship is cheated, and cheated by the very people who are by nature charged with the responsibility of that baby's care and nurture.

Moreover, premarital sex breeds not only unwanted babies, but also remorse and loss of self-respect for the one who participates as well as jealousy and discord for his or her future spouse. Contraceptive measures may reduce the risk of pregnancy, but they don't erase the shame or restore the self-respect. Remember this: if a girl and boy have illicit sex, neither will ever really and truly believe that the other has not or will not do the same with someone else.

Family values are important. Indeed, they are essential to the preservation of a stable social order. Most people know this intuitively. Recent public pronouncements by prominent politicians suggest that pollsters have persuaded them that the prevailing culture wants a country with strong family values.

Chapter Five

The Sources of Moral and Social Values

*T*o understand the need for some system of values is one thing. Of no less importance is to choose the right system of values. That brings us to the question of how to identify sources of values which are best for ourselves, our communities, and our country.

When we talk about values we include moral, social, economic and political values. In some instances they overlap. That is, sometimes moral and social values are the same. Economic and political values often merge in practice. Even so, I think it may be helpful if we focus on each, to some degree at least. By the same token, it will be helpful to deal separately with the sources of these values, their application to our personal lives, and their relationship to our communities and our country.

Some like to call the United States a "Christian nation," but it was not just Christianity alone which shaped the moral elements of the American culture which predominated until the mid-1950s. It was the Judeo-Christian heritage which traces its origin back to the Law of Moses, as interpreted through both Middle Eastern and European religious and secular history. Our American heritage of political values looks back to the English common law, as well as to the "Age of Enlightenment" in western Europe. A sense of individual economic and social freedom was developed by the American colonists and frontiersmen. Holding the whole together was a remarkable sense of community, given that Americans came from several cultures to this "melting pot."

We tend to think of the Mosaic Law as only the Ten Commandments delivered by God to Moses on Mount Sinai.[36] But Moses transmitted to the children of Israel other laws as well: laws of worship, penal laws, dietary laws, and laws of behavior. For examples: the specifications of the tabernacle[37] and the ark[38] were described; the names and times of feasts[39] were given; the death penalty was decreed for murder[40], kidnapping[41], blasphemy[42], adultery[43], and other offenses, including even juvenile delinquency[44]; the dietary laws were detailed[45]; and the laws of behavior set forth a comprehensive system of values which, among other things, proscribed fraud and false measures[46], called for charitable behavior[47] and justice[48], and even required deference to older people.[49]

---

[36] *The Torah* (Second Edition of the translation by The Jewish Publication Society of America, Philadelphia, 1967) Exod. 20: 1-14; Deut. 5: 6-18. All references to *The Torah* are to this translation.

[37] *Torah*, Exod. 25: 8-9; 26; 27: 1-19.

[38] *Torah*, Exod. 25: 10-22.

[39] *Torah*, Exod. 23: 14-17; Deut. 16: 1-17.

[40] *Torah*, Exod. 21: 12, 14; Lev. 24: 17, 21.

[41] *Torah*, Exod. 21: 16.

[42] *Torah*, Lev. 24: 10-16.

[43] *Torah*, Lev. 20: 10.

[44] *Torah*, Exod. 21: 15; Lev. 20: 9; Deut. 21: 18-21.

[45] *Torah*, Lev. 11.

[46] *Torah*, Lev. 19: 11, 13, 35-36.

[47] *Torah*, Exod. 22: 21; Lev. 19: 9-10.

[48] *Torah*, Exod. 23: 6-8; Lev. 19: 15.

[49] *Torah*, Lev. 19: 32.

Beyond those commandments and laws, Moses communicated the two which Jesus later said were the most important. The first was:

> Hear, O Israel! The Lord is our God, the Lord alone.
> You shall love the Lord your God with all your heart
> and with all your soul and with all your might.[50]

And the second:

> Love your neighbor as yourself . . .[51]

And it is clear from the Torah that God meant the Law to be for the good of His people. Moses told them:

> And now, O Israel, what does the Lord your God
> demand of you? Only this: to revere the Lord your
> God, to walk only in His paths, to love Him, and to
> serve the Lord your God with all your heart and
> soul, keeping the Lord's commandments and laws,
> which I enjoin upon you today, for your good.[52]

Their monotheism and the "Law of Moses" set out in the Torah were what set the Jews apart from other peoples; but, to their shame, the Law came to be honored more in the letter than the spirit. Yet, while Jesus spoke of the Pharisees as hypocrites because they ignored the spirit and purpose of the Law in favor of their strained and literal interpretations, He still said:

> Think not that I am come to destroy the law, or the

---

[50] *Torah*, Deut. 6: 5.
[51] *Torah*, Lev. 19: 18.
[52] *Torah*, Deut. 10: 12-13.

prophets, I am not come to destroy, but to fulfill, for
verily I say unto you, till heaven and earth pass, one
jot or one tittle shall in no wise pass from the law...[53]

Jesus taught that the spirit of the Law is love and that
the Law must be interpreted and applied in that spirit. Beyond that, He taught that faith is our nexus with God, Who
Himself is love. Without faith we cannot grasp the meaning
of love. By His resurrection, Jesus provides hope that ultimately good will triumph over evil, and life over death. So
Christian values are grounded in faith, love and hope; and
it is in light of these that Christians understand the Law of
Moses. As Paul wrote to the Romans:

Owe no one anything, except to love one another;
for he who loves his neighbor has fulfilled the law.
The commandments, "You shall not commit adultery, You shall not kill, You shall not steal, You shall
not covet," and any other commandment, are
summed up in this sentence, "You shall love your
neighbor as yourself." Love does no wrong to a
neighbor; therefore love is the fulfilling of the law.[54]

The third of the Western religions, Islam, refers to Jews
as "Followers of the Book," meaning the Torah. So in the
Quràn, which is the sacred book of Islam, it is written:

And most certainly We[55] gave Musa[56] the Book and
We sent apostles after him one after another; and

---

[53] Matt. 5: 17-18.
[54] Rom. 13: 8-10. (RSV)
[55] Meaning Allah, as Muslims refer to God.
[56] Arabic name for Moses.

We gave Isa[57], the son of Marium[58], clear arguments and strengthened him with the holy spirit, . . .[59]

Indeed, the Torah itself is endorsed with specificity, in these words:

Surely We revealed the Taurat[60] in which was guidance and light; . . .[61]

After speaking of the prophets, the Book of Islam continues:

And We send after them in their footsteps Isa, son of Marium, verifying what was before him of the Taurat and We gave him the Injeel[62] in which was guidance and light, and verifying what was before it of Taurat and a guidance and an admonition for those who guard (against evil).[63]

The moral values taught by the Western religions are not a list of "do's and don't's" established for their own sake, but truly expressions of virtue, meant for the good of the individual and the community. Look at what we have come to call the "Beatitudes" delivered during the Sermon on the Mount.[64] Consider them and compare them to "self-esteem," as that concept is taught by the psychologists and social engineers today. One must conclude that values drawn from

---

[57] Arabic name for Jesus.
[58] Arabic name for Mary.
[59] *The Quràn*, (Elmhurst, N.Y.: Tahrike Tarsile Quràn, Inc., Translation by M. H. Shakir, 8th U.S. Ed., 1993) Surah II: 87. All references to The *Quràn* are to this translation.
[60] Arabic name for *Torah*.
[61] *Quràn*, Surah V: 44.
[62] Arabic name for Gospel.
[63] *Quràn*, Surah V: 46.
[64] Matt. 5: 3-12.

the Beatitudes are far more difficult in practice than the self-centered ideas related to "self-esteem." But the former lead to peace, both in one's own mind and in his relationships with others, while "self-esteem" leads to dependency, frustration and conflict with others, who themselves pursue their own "self-esteem."

Now we can see why Jesus gave us the "Golden Rule" and said:

> Therefore all things whatsoever ye would that men should do to you, do ye even so to them; for this is the law and the prophets.[65]

This is why Paul said in his letter to the Romans, "love does no wrong to a neighbor; therefore love is the fulfilling of the law."[66]

While the "Golden Rule" sums up "the Law and the Prophets," we daily deal with decisions in circumstances wholly unknown two thousand years ago, or even earlier in the twentieth century. We need guidance in specific terms, which we can more easily relate to those choices with which we are confronted. So it is that today's priests interpret the Scriptures in terms of today's circumstances, and today's lawyers likewise the law. In doing so, all of us must be careful to not forget the spirit of love, truth, justice and mercy. If we forget the spirit, we deserve the same indictment leveled by Jesus at the scribes and Pharisees.[67]

Please understand that my reference to changing times and circumstances is not meant to suggest that all values are simply "relative" and none absolute. Some are relative. Jesus taught that to heal the sick is of greater importance

---

[65] Matt. 7: 12.
[66] Rom. 13: 10 (RSV).
[67] Matt. 15: 7-9; 23: 23-28.

than to keep the Sabbath, saying "The Sabbath was made for man, and not man for the Sabbath."[68] But there are absolutes. "You shall not murder. You shall not commit adultery. You shall not steal."[69] There are no times or circumstances to excuse a violation of these. Therefore, when He was asked which of the commandments was the greatest, Jesus spoke of their purpose rather than their terms. He told them:

> The first is, "Hear, O Israel: The Lord our God, the Lord is one: and you shall love the Lord your God with all your heart, and with all your soul, and with all your mind, and with all your strength." The second is this, "You shall love your neighbor as yourself." There is no other commandment greater than these.[70]

Our values and virtue drawn from them must begin with these two, which are the purpose and foundation of all else. In all cultures and in every generation, the standard of values and their relative importance should be determined in light of these two principles: love of God and love of neighbor. Concentrate on them. If you really love God and your neighbor, you won't be far from goodness, according to moral and social values as well as civil and criminal law.

Paul Prather, sometime religion writer for the *Lexington Herald-Leader* recently wrote that:

> A great many folks of all persuasions long for a cultural rebirth of honesty, sexual fidelity, parental responsibility, hard work, faith and self-reliance.[71]

---

[68] Mark 2: 27.
[69] Exod. 20: 13-15 (NAS).
[70] Mark 12: 29-31 (RSV).
[71] Paul Prather, "Churches Must Face Issues . . . Head-on", *Lexington* (KY) *Herald-Leader*, October 1, 1994.

These are values taught by Moses and the prophets. Prather's is not the only voice raised in this effort. Judge Dennis quoted from a policy statement issued by the Free Congress Research and Education Foundation as follows:

> There is a necessary, unbreakable, and causal relationship between traditional Western, Judeo-Christian values, definitions of right and wrong, ways of thinking and ways of living — the parameters of Western culture — and the secular success of Western societies: their prosperity, their liberties, and the opportunities they offer their citizens to lead fulfilling, rewarding lives. If the former are abandoned, the latter will be lost.[72]

Does all this mean that we must look to some electronic evangelist or Church hierarchy to dictate our moral and social values? No. Does this mean that we in America should have a theocracy, as in Muslim countries? No. Does this mean that a priest or preacher or mullah or rabbi should write our laws for us? No. Does this suggest some breach in the wall of separation between church and state? No. Suggestions that moral values have a place in the life of our country and that moral values are drawn from religions close the minds of some of our fellow citizens, who appear to prefer hedonism and libertarianism to the moral and social values which once guided Americans, simply because they come from the Western religions. They need not be afraid. We can take the best of values from religious sources without requiring fellow citizens to accept the religions as such. Indeed, in his postscript to *The Culture of Disbelief*, Yale law professor Stephen L. Carter wrote: "This is the principal distinction I have defended in this book: we must be

---

[72] Dennis, *Trial* article, p. 56.

able, in our secular society, to distinguish a critique of the content of a belief from a critique of its source."[73] Nor should we ourselves have to become irreligious to preserve America. Those of us who take God seriously are entitled to voice our values in "the public square."[74]

The Apostle taught that salvation for Christians is by faith and not by works;[75] he wrote that the Law had been fulfilled in Jesus;[76] he held that "all things are lawful";[77] and he wrote about freedom in Christ.[78] But he was quick to say that this does not license misbehavior.[79] Instead, he wrote beautifully of values, saying:

> But the fruit of the Spirit is love, joy, peace, patience, kindness, goodness, faithfulness, gentleness, self-control; against such there is no law.[80]

And:

> Finally, brethren, whatever is true, whatever is honorable, whatever is just, whatever is pure, whatever is lovely, whatever is gracious, if there is any excellence, if there is anything worthy of praise, think about these things.[81]

How can anybody object to these moral and social values, even if they are found in the Bible?

---

[73] Stephen L. Carter, *The Culture of Disbelief* (New York: Doubleday-Anchor Books, 1994), p. 277.

[74] Ibid., p. 214.

[75] Rom. 3: 21-25, 28; Gal. 2: 15-16; Eph. 2: 8-9.

[76] Rom. 10: 4; Gal. 3: 24-26.

[77] I Cor. 6: 12, 10: 23-24.

[78] Gal. 5: 1.

[79] Rom. 6: 1-2, 12-16; Gal. 5: 13-14.

[80] Gal. 5: 22-23. (RSV)

[81] Phil. 4: 8. (RSV)

Apart from religion, we find moral values in philosophy. Philosophers have wrestled with these issues; not that they were critical of goodness so much as they sought its rationale. In the fourth century before Christ, Aristotle taught that "it is a man's virtuous activities that constitute his happiness and their opposites that constitute his misery."[82] He said that "the happy life is a life of virtue."[83] According to Aristotle, virtue is a matter of one's choice. Indeed, he said that, "the virtues are matters of deliberate purpose, or require deliberate purpose."[84] "Virtue then is a state of deliberate moral purpose. . ."[85] he wrote; adding "moral purpose is clearly something voluntary."[86]

I have told you that, in large measure, your life will become the product of your choices; and you might remember that Aristotle said, "it is in our power to be good or wicked."[87]

Among the virtues of which Aristotle writes at some length are courage[88], temperance[89], liberality[90], magnificence[91], high-mindedness[92], and truth[93].

Aristotle also wrote of wisdom, prudence and justice. In *Nicomachean Ethics*, he said that, "Wisdom therefore will be a union of intuitive reason (which he discussed in Book VI, Chapter 12) and scientific knowledge (which he discussed

[82] Aristotle, *On Man In The Universe*, Classics Club, ed. by Louise Ropes Loomis (Roslyn, N. Y.: Walter J. Black, Inc., 1943). *Nichomachean Ethics*, Book I, Chapter 11, p. 96.
[83] Ibid., Book X, Chapter 6, p. 232.
[84] Ibid., Book II, Chapter 4, p. 105.
[85] Ibid., Book II, Chapter 6, p. 108.
[86] Ibid., Book III, Chapter 4, p. 117.
[87] Ibid., Book III, Chapter 7, p. 122.
[88] Ibid., Book III, Chapters 9-11.
[89] Ibid., Book III, Chapters 13-14.
[90] Ibid., Book IV, Chapters 1-3.
[91] Ibid., Book IV, Chapters 4-6.
[92] Ibid., Book IV, Chapters 7-9.
[93] Ibid., Book IV, Chapter 13.

in Book VI, Chapter 3)"[94]. He wrote, "goodness in the strict sense is impossible without prudence, and prudence without moral virtue,"[95] going on to say "for prudence determines the right end, and virtue makes us act for the attainment of the end."[96] Finally, in writing of justice, Aristotle said:

> Justice then in this form is complete virtue, though not in an absolute sense, still so in relation to one's neighbors . . . It is complete because he who possesses it can practice virtue not merely in himself but towards his neighbors, and many people can be good at home but not in their relations with their neighbors . . . For this same reason, justice alone of the virtues seems to mean the good of the other fellow, since it implies a relation to other people and works for the interest of someone else, whether our ruler or a simple fellow citizen. . . .
>
> Justice therefore, in this sense of the word, is not a part of virtue but the whole of virtue; . . . They are the same, but the idea of them is different; the state of character which, if regarded in its relation to others, is justice, if regarded absolutely as a moral state, is virtue.[97]

Aristotle even wrote about the social values, specifically friendliness[98], good temper[99], truthfulness[100], and wit[101]. It

---

[94] Ibid., Book VI, Chapter 7, p. 174.
[95] Ibid., Book VI, Chapter 13, p. 177.
[96] Ibid., Book VI, Chapter 13, p. 178.
[97] Ibid., Book V, Chapter 3, pp. 156-157.
[98] Ibid., Books VIII and IX, pp. 194-223.
[99] Ibid., Book IV, Chapter 11, pp. 148-149.
[100] Ibid., Book IV, Chapter 13, pp. 150-152.
[101] Ibid., Book IV, Chapter 14, pp. 152-153.

should not be forgotten that wit and laughter are appropriate when, as this philosopher teaches, they do not go beyond or fall short of the "mean." He puts it is this language:

> Now those who carry humor beyond the proper
> limit are vulgar clowns, for their hearts are set on
> humor at any cost, and they aim rather at raising
> a laugh than at using decent language and not giv-
> ing pain to the butt of their fun. On the other hand,
> those who never themselves make a joke and are
> indignant with everybody who does, are said to be
> boorish and crude. People whose fun is in good taste
> are called quick-witted, a name which implies the
> happy turns of their art, . . .[102]

As Aristotle suggests, without laughter life would be dour
and foreboding. Laughter is healthy, both physically and
mentally.

There are additional sources of good values which are
close at hand. The Boy Scouts of America inculcate worthwhile moral and social values in their members. For example,
the Boy Scout oath is as follows:

> On my honor I will do my best to do my duty to
> God and my country and to obey the Scout law; to
> help other people at all times; to keep myself physi-
> cally strong, mentally awake, and morally straight.

The twelve points of the Boy Scout law constitute a
simple but thorough listing of worthwhile values. It says,
"A Scout is trustworthy, loyal, helpful, friendly, courteous,
kind, obedient, cheerful, thrifty, brave, clean and reverent."

---

[102] Ibid., Book IV, Chapter 14, p. 152.

The Creed of the Shriners is not secret. It binds members of that fraternal organization to wholesome moral and social values in the following language:

Shriners believe in God and that He created man to serve His purposes, among which is service to others in His name. We believe that care for the less fortunate, especially children who suffer from burns and crippling disease, is our institutional calling.

We are patriots, each willing to serve his country with fidelity and courage. We cherish independence under law and freedom with responsibility.

We honor family. We respect our parents, wives and children. We should instill in our children the tenets of this creed, and the heritage from which it emanates. As individuals we pledge ourselves to integrity, virtue, and nobility of character. Our intentions will be honorable, our relationships will be trustworthy and our spirits forgiving of each other.

As brothers we offer each other fraternal affection and respect. Together we will support each other in adherence to this creed, so that we and our communities will be the better because of our fraternity and its principles.

As Shriners we look beyond ourselves to serve the needs of others, especially children who cannot help themselves. We believe Shriners Hospitals to be the world's greatest philanthropy, and we covenant with each other to support its "temples of mercy" with spirit, time, talent, and means.

Of course, the behavior of Boy Scouts does not always comport with the Boy Scout oath and the Boy Scout law. Neither do Shriners always live lives consistent with the Shriners Creed. Boy Scouts and Shriners are like the Apostle, who wrote:

> I do not understand my own actions. For I do not do what I want, but I do the very thing I hate. . . . For I do not do the good I want, but the evil I do not want is what I do.[103]

But remember this: the fact that all of us sometimes miss the mark and violate our own values does not mean that the values are to blame. Better to set high standards and sometimes fail to reach them than to set none, or to set standards so low as to have no challenge.

Moreover, to simply read about the standards of the Torah, the New Testament, the Quràn, or some organization is not enough. Credit is earned only by conforming to high standards after having internalized them and made them a part of one's self. William J. Bennett, after serving in Cabinet-level positions under two Presidents, put it this way:

> I have seen men and women of integrity in the House and Senate, in the Judiciary and Executive branches and outside of government, in the press. They demonstrate what should be obvious but, like many great truths, is often overlooked: character is inextricably linked to, is part and parcel of, the individual, not his party or institution; it is something a man or woman either has or lacks. You don't get it from membership; like so many other things, you get it from within.[104]

---

[103] Rom. 7: 15, 19. (RSV)
[104] William J. Bennett, *The De-valuing of America* (New York: Simon & Schuster, Touchstone, 1994), p. 233.

Bennett describes his *The Book of Virtues*[105] as "a 'how to' book for moral literacy"[106] and classifies the virtues as self-discipline, compassion, responsibility, friendship, work, courage, perseverance, honesty, loyalty and faith.

Moral values are alike in different countries and cultures. So are many of the social values, although they are manifested in different ways. The differences are related to different cultural backgrounds, sometimes running back for hundreds of years. Social values may be of less importance than moral, political and economic values; but they alleviate tension in social situations and put everybody at ease, because they are the basis for expected behavior and constitute the cultural norm. Social values are directly related to cultures, and will be discussed in that section of this book. It is sufficient here to say that they include styles, manners, customs, courtesy and "class." They are essentially innocent and not of sufficient consequence to warrant enactment into law, but they strengthen the social fabric. Indeed, disregard for the social values creates an atmosphere of tension and can lead to rejection of the miscreant by social traditionalists. Thus, the time-honored expression: "When in Rome, do as the Romans do."

Study all these sources of good and worthwhile moral and social values and you will see that your life, as well as the lives of others, will be the better for it if you make them a part of yourself.

---

[105] William J. Bennett, *The Book of Virtues* (New York: Simon & Schuster, 1993).
[106] Ibid., p. 11.

Chapter Six

The Sources of Political Values and the Rule of Law

*M*any Americans take for granted our unique heritage of political values, apparently under the mistaken impression that it has always been thus. Not so! Not so!

With one or two limited exceptions for short periods of time, it is only in the last 200 years and only in a very few countries that the masses of the people have had and exercised political power. By and large, over the 5,000 years of recorded history, only the privileged few had any influence whatever on the political systems, which held the great majority of the people in servitude to the elite. Politics plainly reflected the economic, military and religious power of the day. Most of the people were illiterate peasants, vassals or serfs. Governments were theocratic, autocratic, or both. Kings attributed to God their right to rule, calling it "the Divine Right of Kings." This melded Church and state, each of which supported the other or used the other in order to gain and maintain power.

In our own history we look back to our English heritage for the Rule of Law, which puts even Princes and Presidents beneath and subject to the law. Likewise, it limits the legislative branch to enact only laws which are consistent with the Constitution. It provides what we call a government of laws, and not of men. No man or group of men is above the law, or not subject to it.

We Americans have a tendency to take for granted our form of government, because every generation now alive has experienced nothing else. But we enjoy a unique and precious heritage. This heritage is unknown in most countries of the world, where the rich and powerful can ignore the law with impunity.

The Rule of Law had its first written expression in the Magna Carta, which was signed by King John in 1215 for the honefit of the English nobles It provided for what we now call "due process of law." But the Magna Carta was not self-executing, and it was meaningful only insofar as the courts enforced its terms as a part of what had come to be known as the common law. By way of explanation, the common law is case-made law. Unlike statutory law which is enacted by the legislative branch, common law is developed case by case as judges write opinions giving the reasons for their decisions.

When Queen Elizabeth I died in the spring of 1603, the Tudor line ended and James I, a Scot of the Stuart family, became King of England. It has been said that, "Fate could scarcely have sent a more inappropriate monarch than James to rule England at this juncture."[107] Claiming to be "King by divine hereditary right" and "God's lieutenant upon earth" James I viewed Parliament as nothing but his rubber stamp.[108] Moreover, he insisted that the crown embodied the law, so that he was not bound by the common law of

---

[107] F. E. Halliday, *England, a Concise History* (London: Thames and Hudson, Rev. Ed., 1989), p. 109.
[108] Ibid., p. 110.

England. This set the stage for a great struggle of which we are principal beneficiaries.

In her superb biography of Sir Edward Coke, Catherine Drinker Bowen wrote of his regard for the Magna Carta as follows:

> . . . Any second-term Templar could recite the pertinent chapter of Magna Carta: . . . "no Freeman shall be taken or imprisoned or be disseised[109] of his freehold or liberties but by lawful judgment of his peers or by the law of the land." "Upon this chapter" Coke wrote, "as out of a roote, many fruitful branches of the law of England have sprung.
>
> "A Freeman may have habeas corpus out of the king, upon which writ the gaoler[110] must return by whom he was committed and the cause of his imprisonment." So the great Bracton had said in Henry III's time, and so Edward Coke believed. There were no bounds to his conviction. . . .[111]

It was this great lawyer whom James I appointed Chief Justice of the Court of Common Pleas in 1606 and who thereupon became an unparalleled advocate for the common law.

It was not long until Coke earned the enmity of the Lord Chancellor and Archbishop Bancroft by issuing writs of prohibition from the common pleas court to the ecclesiastical courts, challenging the jurisdiction of the latter over any controversies not clearly unrelated to temporal matters. The Archbishop appealed to the King, who called Coke be-

---

[109] This word means dispossessed.
[110] This word means jailer.
[111] Catherine Drinker Bowen, *The Lion and the Throne* (New York: Little, Brown and Company, 1956), p. 65.

fore the Privy Council. There, in November 1608, Coke told the King that "Bracton saith that the King should not be under man, but under God and the Laws." The King was incensed, but Sir Robert Cecil intervened and Coke was spared a cell in the Tower. On the "next morning a new prohibition, under Coke's seal, went out to High Commission from the Court of Common Pleas."[112]

Nor was that the end of Coke's influence on the common law. Two years later, in Bonham's Case, Coke ruled that a statute authorizing the Royal College of Physicians to fine physicians and then itself receive half of each fine collected, made the College a judge in its own case so that the statute of incorporation should be disallowed. He wrote: "that in many cases the common law will control acts of Parliament and some times adjudge them to be utterly void; for when an Act of Parliament is against common right and reason, or repugnant, or impossible to be performed, the common law will control it and adjudge such Act to be void."[113]

In 1628 Coke was a member of the House of Commons in "an extraordinary Parliament, one of the two most celebrated in English history."[114] By then, Charles I was King. To support an unpopular war with France, he sought "subsidies" from the people and imprisoned those who refused to pay, even though Parliament had not approved the levy. In spite of his painful reluctance to do so, Charles called a Parliament. Led by Coke and others, all at the risk of their own liberty, that Parliament adopted a "Petition of Right" to which the King finally acceded and by which the writ of habeas corpus was again confirmed, and the principle that any tax or loan must be authorized by Parliament was reestablished.[115]

---

[112] Ibid., p. 306.
[113] Ibid., p. 315.
[114] Ibid., p. 481.
[115] Ibid., pp. 473-504 ; and see Halliday, *England, a History*, p. 115.

We likewise revere Thomas Erskine, who freed the bar from the bench when in 1784 he stood before a judge who threatened him with punishment for contempt of court and said, "I stand here as an advocate for a brother citizen . . . I know my duty as well as Your Lordship knows yours. I shall not alter my conduct."[116]

Former Supreme Court Justice Oliver Wendell Holmes, Jr., wrote the authoritative American work on case-made law, titled *The Common Law*.[117] He traced the common law from its roots, then went on to write:

> The foregoing history, apart from the purposes for which it has been given, well illustrates the paradox of form and substance in the development of law. In form its growth is logical. The official theory is that each new decision follows syllogistically from existing precedents. But . . . precedents survive in the law long after the use they once served is at an end and the reason for them has been forgotten . . .

> On the other hand, in substance the growth of the law is legislative . . . The very considerations which judges most rarely mention, and always with an apology, are the secret root from which the law draws all the juices of life. I mean, of course, considerations of what is expedient for the community concerned. Every important principle which is developed by litigation is in fact and at bottom the result of more or less definitely understood views of public policy; . . . And as the law is administered by able and experienced men, who know too much

---

[116] Lloyd Paul Stryker, *For the Defense* (Garden City, N.Y.: Doubleday & Company, 1947), pp. 131-132.
[117] Holmes, Jr., *The Common Law*, 1881.

to sacrifice good sense to a syllogism, it will be found that, when ancient rules maintain themselves in the way that has been and will be shown in this book, new reasons more fitted to the time have been found for them, . . .[118]

So then Holmes says:

It remains to be proved that, while the terminology of morals is still retained, and while the law does still and always, in a certain sense, measure legal liability by moral standards, it nevertheless, by the very necessity of its nature, is continually transmuting those moral standards into external or objective ones, from which the actual guilt of the party concerned is wholly eliminated.[119]

All of this is in demonstration of Holmes' principal thesis which is that: "The life of the law has not been logic; it has been experience."[120]

The English common law differs considerably from what came to be called "civil" or "continental" law, the roots of which were in the Roman law and especially the Justinian Code. One of the obvious differences is in trial by jury, which developed in England. On the continent, judges hear and decide issues of fact in an inquisitorial fashion, participating far more in questioning witnesses than do judges in the common law countries, where issues of fact are decided by juries.

Freedom of the press in America came by way of the trial of Peter Zenger. He was represented by Andrew Hamilton, who fashioned his defense after the William Penn case and

---

[118] Ibid., pp. 35-37.
[119] Ibid., p. 38.
[120] Ibid., p. 1.

Bushell's Case, in which the Penn jurors were released on habeas corpus and the judge's power to direct their verdict on matters of fact was ended.[121] You will see many examples of unfair, irresponsible and inaccurate reporting in the media, which is to be deplored; but without freedom of the press a country cannot be free.

While the proponents of "political correctness" would like us to ignore the fact that all of these freedoms and the Rule of Law came to us from England, that country was in fact their source. Indeed, the civilization of which we are heirs began in the Fertile Crescent at the eastern end of the Mediterranean Sea in the fourth millennium B.C. and through the intervening fifty centuries made its way through Asia Minor and Europe to the United States.

We have a constitution which is designed to protect the people from those in power. Other countries have constitutions; but in most of them the people have no means to enforce their constitutional rights. Not so here in America. Our constitution is an effective shield used by an independent legal profession to protect the people's rights. Indeed, we sometimes see cases in which the overzealous demand is for virtually absolute individual freedom. But freedom is not absolute. It is relative to the rights of others; and, therefore, to the interests of the whole community. Freedom is inextricably linked to responsibility. No community can accord its people absolute freedom; nor endure if the only ties among its people are the "rights" each demands of the others.

Our country is a democratic republic. Each of us who chooses to do so, may vote for the elected officials who operate our government, including its titular head, the President. So those who govern are chosen by those whom they govern.

We claim a right to vote. Remembering the relation-

---

[121] Julius J. Marke, *Vignettes of Legal History* (South Hackensack, N.J.: Fred B. Rothman & Co., 1965), pp. 217-240.

ship between rights and responsibilities, you will understand that participatory democracy casts upon voters the responsibility of being informed. As in other areas, choices should be based upon information; and here, information as to both the issues and the candidates. In order for voters to have appropriate information upon which they can make good political choices, it is essential that they have full and fair reporting by the news media which, in turn, must be given the freedom of speech which will permit expression of unpopular opinions, as well as popular opinions. As in other cases, with this right to free speech comes a correlative responsibility to report fully, fairly and accurately.

Likewise, politicians have the responsibility to be truthful with their constituents and to avoid half-truth and demagoguery. If the people cannot trust those in politics to tell the whole truth, democracy is jeopardized, both by misinformation and by the people's cynicism.

One of the important predicates for a successful democracy is a literate electorate; hence the need for a good system of public education in a democratic republic. Public education must teach our American heritage to succeeding generations. A federal republic such as ours can continue to flourish only if the people shall have learned about the heritage in which it developed, and the need to keep a watchful eye out for those who would pervert it to serve purposes of their own.

In his insightful critique of modern American education,[122] Professor Bloom persuasively explains how teachers, disdaining values and encouraging only an "openness" which tolerates any kind of behavior, have themselves brought on "the collapse of the entire American educational structure."[123] He poses the question: "But when there are no shared goals or vision of the public good, is the social

---

[122] Bloom, *Closing of the American Mind*.
[123] Ibid., p. 321.

contract any longer possible?"[124] One wonders how democracy can long endure without a commonly accepted system of values; much less how, as some seem to believe, it can be planted in countries which have no heritage or sense of the Rule of Law.

Not only those who devote their careers to public service, but likewise those who vote should have been taught something about the different political and economic theories upon which the major political parties base their campaigns and justify their actions when in power. This is not for the sake of argument, but because those theories form the premises for the positions taken by each party; and that is true even though the real reasons for their actions are not always stated or revealed.

An elementary fact, often overlooked, is that public affairs involve both politics and economics. The two are "joined at the hip." They are interdependent. Therefore, those who make the laws take some actions grounded in politics, other actions grounded in economics, and still other actions grounded in both politics and economics. This book is not meant to be a textbook for either economics or political science. Nevertheless, it will be better understood if the distinction is made between the two principal theories of politics and the two principal theories of economics now prevailing in most of the world. Elsewhere we consider those of economics, so we shall turn to those of politics.

While both systems can be turned into despotism by ignorance or corruption of the Rule of Law, the two principal political systems are the monarchy and the democratic republic. In the one, power is in the hands of the king; in the other, power is in the people. Democracy was only a dream until the people of the United States organized a great

---

[124] Ibid., p. 27.

experiment in America, and established a constitutional democratic republic under the Rule of Law. While the words are now used worldwide, in some places a nominal republic is actually controlled by a dictator. There elections are *pro forma* rather than free. On the other hand, in some countries the monarchy is only symbolic and the reality is a republican government; so there the people actually have power.

There is a practical limit to the amount of taxes a government may levy on its people, so nations as well as individuals have limited financial resources. When governments spend more than they receive in taxes, they create budget deficits and debt. Within limits, national governments can issue bonds and other instruments of debt. But government debt tends to cause inflation, with its risk of either economic or political collapse. Therefore, repeated deficits and increasing public debt is very dangerous. Governments can go broke. Some have. So long as government has only limited financial resources, the political system determines the allocation of those resources. So it can be said that politics is economics.

As some say, "the golden rule means that those with the gold make the rules." It is only in the last two centuries that a somewhat different situation has obtained, — and this primarily in the United States. Here we have seen most people accept the view that the Rule of Law has as part of its purpose to help those who cannot help themselves, — even at the expense of the rich and powerful. Such an idea could not become law absent the vesting of power in those who are not the rich.

Politicians speak of freedom, and often cloak a hidden agenda under that term. But pure freedom is anarchy, which produces chaos. In any social order, there will be tension between individual freedoms on the one hand, and the creation and enforcement of standards for the benefit of the community on the other hand. Indeed, one of the community standards is that of individual freedom. Another, which is quite as difficult to define and implement, is the limitation of individual freedom in such ways as are necessary for the common good.

In public affairs, as well as in private affairs, there must be recognized and accepted standards of morals and ethics. Unprincipled voters may be worse than uninformed voters; and unprincipled politicians are the greatest threat to good government.

Before you align yourself with a political party, give the matter some study. For example, the parties differ as to whether greater good can be done by larger or lesser control by government. With which do you agree? They also disagree as to how far a political system should go in redistributing the wealth and earnings of its citizens, through the power of taxation, so that those who are affluent are compelled by government to help care for those who are perceived to be in need. With which do you agree? Some politicians will try to confuse the issues, or to state them in unfair terms. Listen to them with an analytical ear. Remember this: you must think. Don't accept bad ideas dressed up in euphemisms. Make your decision as to which of the two major parties best reflects your own thinking as to both its political and economic principles.

After a recent election, the media complained bitterly about "negative" campaigning. They say that political races are about issues. They are. But that is not the whole story. That is only half the truth. Political offices are held by people, some good and some bad. Some officeholders can be trusted, and some not. Campaigns can help to tell which of them tell the truth. Character and integrity are properly to be revealed and considered.

Finally, party loyalty should not be absolute. There are times when one should support a candidate because of specific issues or because of the personal character of that candidate or his opponent. In those times, do what is best for your community and your country, even if it means voting for a candidate of another party.

Chapter Seven

The Sources of Economic Values

*E*conomics is defined as "the science that deals with the production, distribution, and consumption of commodities."[125] I prefer to think of economics as a study of methods by which finite or limited resources are allocated among people and communities. Here, by "resources" I mean collectively the people, materials, facilities and money utilized to meet a need. In the nature of things, there are never enough resources to accomplish everything which everybody would like to see accomplished. So resources are limited or finite. An economic system is essential.

Over the course of history there have developed two principal economic systems which, in their pure forms, are called capitalism and socialism. By one or the other, or by a combination of both, the needs of production, distribution, services and finance are met.

---

[125] *The American Heritage Dictionary*, 2nd College Edition (Boston: Houghton Mifflin Co., 1991).

Free enterprise, as capitalism is often called, is based on trust; that is, upon confidence that each of us can be trusted in commercial affairs. It also has as an essential premise the belief that human nature is in large measure selfish and acquisitive. Moreover, it proceeds from the observation that talents and resources are not equally divided among all people; and that, even if they were, the talented and most industrious would soon have a larger share than the dull or lazy.

Thus has arisen the system through which those with greater resources make investments so that those with greater talents may have opportunities.

Suppose you have an opportunity to go to college, to build a home, or to start a business but you don't have the money to do so. Capitalism provides a solution to your problem. A lender, believing that he can trust you, will lend you the money so that you can take advantage of your opportunity. His risk is your willingness and ability to repay the loan when it becomes due. His payment to assume that risk and for your use of his money over the time you borrow it is the interest which he charges. So opportunity and acceptance of risk drive the system in such a fashion that both the lender and the borrower can profit from the transaction; and in a relationship created between two private interests.[126]

A similar relationship is created when the person with resources buys a partnership interest or capital stock in a business managed by someone else. This kind of investment is another example of risk creating opportunity, with the aim that both the risk-taker and the business will profit by their relationship.

---

[126] Peter Drucker says that "we are currently living through . . . a transformation (which) is creating the post-capitalistic society;" and that it proceeds in part from "capitalism without capitalists", i.e., a concentration of capital in institutional investors such as pension funds. Peter Drucker, *Post-capitalist Society* (New York: HarperCollins Publishers, Harper Business, 1993), pp. 1, 74-75.

When the system is operating efficiently, almost everybody who wants to work is gainfully employed. So, even though the degrees of benefit may not be equal, through free enterprise there is a distribution of resources which provides benefits to everybody.

The painful problem of economics is that there are always the rich and the poor. As Jesus said, "Ye have the poor with you always."[127] This is true because, in spite of neverending assurance to the contrary, people are not equal. They are not equal in abilities. They are not equal in resources. They are not equal in circumstances. They are equal in the sight of God; but they are not equal in this world.

From the very earliest times, after men turned from hunting for their food to growing it, those who owned the land were an elite who, by the power of their wealth, controlled the whole society. Dr. Norman F. Cantor calls this "the domination of a landed aristocracy" which, he says, "is one of the fundamental facts and continuing conditions of the history of western civilization."[128] Dr. Cantor writes:

> In the ancient world, in Egypt and Mesopotamia, the social structure was justified on religious grounds. It was God's plan for the world — God's will — and acceptance of the social forms was a religious duty. Medieval men inherited that attitude and built upon it. They had more difficulty than the Egyptians, in doing so however, because certain strains within Christianity were incompatible with the ancient system. There is an egalitarian strain in the Bible (particularly in the Hebrew prophets and in the New Testament), for example,

---

[127] Mark 14: 7.
[128] Norman F. Cantor, *The Civilization of the Middle Ages* (New York: HarperCollins Publishers, Harper Perennial, 1993), p. 3.

that runs counter to the ancient traditions of exploitation and domination.[129]

There is nothing new about exploitation of the poor and
domination by the rich.
    We know that in ancient times men first settled in small
villages. Cities were not developed until transportation was
available to move food from the fields into the cities; and
larger cities came only when markets were established for
the distribution of food. Professor William H. McNeill explains it in this fashion:

> All cities, of course, had to import food and often
> found it hard to find sufficient grain in the imme-
> diate hinterland. Long before a market system
> could be relied on to supply cities from afar, a few
> great capital cities depended on food coming from
> relatively great distances in the economically un-
> requited form of tribute and taxes. . . .

> It is no exaggeration to say that the cultural splen-
> dor and military formidability of early civilizations
> depended on the concentration of food and other
> commodities at court and temple centers by dint of
> exercise of direct command. The very notion of sepa-
> rate, autonomous civilizations registers this early
> division of labor, whereby the many toiled in the
> fields while a privileged few consumed the yield of
> rents and taxes and experimented with all the arts
> of civilization . . .[130]

---

[129] Ibid., p. 5.
[130] William H. McNeill, *The Rise of the West* (Chicago: The University of
    Chicago Press, 1991), pp. xxii, xxiii.

Then came the industrial revolution followed by what C. P. Snow calls the "scientific revolution."[131] Snow says:

> . . . The main issue is that the people in the industrialized countries are getting richer, and those in the nonindustrialized countries are at best standing still: so that the gap between the industrialized countries and the rest is widening every day. On the world scale this is the gap between the rich and the poor.[132]

J. M. Roberts sees it the same way. He writes:

> A rough division can be drawn in all parts of the world between rich and poor nations in which the disparity since 1945 has grown more and more marked. This is not because the poor have grown poorer, but because the rich have grown much richer. . . .[133]

In an ideal society, the rich would take care of the poor through adequate wages for their labor or through charity for the helpless. But generally the rich won't do that. Some rich people are marvelous philanthropists. Others are not. Because most of us have come to believe that society has the responsibility to care for those who cannot care for themselves, government now steps in and taxes the rich to provide for the poor. This creates new and different problems, of course; and perhaps as many as it solves. Yet some redistribution of the wealth is essential in order that the poor

---

[131] C. P. Snow, *The Two Cultures* (Cambridge: Cambridge University Press, Canto Ed., 1993), p. 29.

[132] Ibid., p. 41.

[133] J. M. Roberts, *History of the World* (London: Penguin Books, 1990), p. 916.

and the helpless do not starve. Serious and valid questions arise as to the methods by which this is done.

An op-ed piece recently published in *The Lexington Herald-Leader*[134] calls the free enterprise system a "competitive market economy." Michael Fogler then says:

> The problem is that a competitive market economy — by definition — isn't fair; and it can't be made fair, either.
>
> By definition, this way of economics produces some people as winners, others as losers. That's what competition is.

The writer suggests instead that:

> . . . we would have to look in a new direction: cooperative economics. Helping and serving one another. Giving to one another. Coming up with ways of living — more happily than we are now — on less. It's possible; and the cooperative paradigm carries with it at least the potential for fairness.

He concedes that "many may consider these ideas to be hopelessly idealistic and 'polyanna-ish' (sic)." Of course we do, because his ideas are wholly unrealistic. They sound good, but they take no account of human nature. All too few human beings are the nice, sharing people Fogler sees in his utopia. Many will not obey the law, much less live by the moral and ethical values needed for his visionary community. If fewer than all are sharing, helping and serving one another, Fogler's "cooperative economics" is nonsense. It is

[134] Michael Fogler, "Lexington Can Escape the Competitive 'Prison,'" *The Lexington* (KY) *Herald-Leader*, July 9, 1995, p. E3.

simply a euphemism for socialism, and history furnishes no example of its success in this world.

Socialism makes a continuous effort to redistribute wealth, regardless of risk or effort. Socialism takes its cue from Karl Marx, who said that an economic system should take "from each according to his abilities, (and give) to each according to his needs." The economic relationship created by socialism is a relationship established through government. Because it purports to treat people as economic equals, it is contrary to human nature. It therefore requires the force of government to compel redistribution of the wealth through taxes on the "haves" and government-controlled benefits for the "have nots." In its pure form, it cannot long endure unless the government is a totalitarian state. This is true because it must counter the selfishness of human nature and impliedly deny the fact that people are different. The combination of a socialistic economy and an authoritarian government is enough to bring down both, as we have recently seen in eastern Europe.

In the real world, neither socialism nor capitalism is pure. There are areas of each in which principles of the other must be utilized to preserve the social compact.

In a free enterprise system there is some voluntary redistribution of wealth by way of charity, and charitable means of sharing wealth in the United States is without parallel anywhere in the world. Professor Drucker has directed attention toward what he calls a purely American "counterculture of values," describing it as:

> . . . the counterculture of the non-business, non-government, "human-change agencies," the non-profit organizations of the so-called third sector,[135]

---

[135] Peter Drucker, *The New Realities* (New York: Harper & Row, 1989), p. 195.

among which he counts hospitals, schools, large philan-
thropic organizations, community service groups, churches
and cultural organizations. "Their unpaid 'volunteers' are
the largest single group in the American workforce."[136] In
the context of his book, the term "counterculture of values"
is used to describe institutions served by people who do not
seek economic gain by their service. Indeed, they are motivated by the very values which drive the culture we endorse.

Milton Friedman is a Nobel prize-winning Professor of
Economics and highly regarded advocate of free enterprise
and capitalism. He wrote a *Newsweek* column which was
later republished in his book[137]. In it he answered fellow
columnist Shana Alexander, who had written "Access to food,
clothing, shelter, and medical care is a basic human right. When
lawmakers attempt to convert welfare into workfare . . . this is
less conversion than perversion of that basic idea," by himself writing:

> If I have the "right" to food in this sense, someone
> must have the obligation to provide it. Just who is
> that? If it is Ms. Alexander, does that not convert
> her into my slave? Nothing is changed by assign-
> ing the "right" to the "poor". Their "right" is mean-
> ingless unless it is combined with the power to force
> others to provide the goods to which Ms. Alexander
> believes they are entitled.

This is clearly unacceptable. But neither can we
rely solely on the "right to access" in the first sense.
Protecting that right fully would reduce poverty
and destitution drastically. But there would still

---

[136] Ibid., p. 187.
[137] Milton Friedman, *There's No Such Thing as a Free Lunch* (Chicago:
Open Court Publishing Co., 1975).

remain people who, through no fault of their own, because of accidents of birth, or illness, or whatever, were unable to earn what the rest of us would regard as an acceptable minimum income. I believe that the best, though admittedly imperfect, solution for such residual hardship would be voluntary action on the part of the rest of us to assist our less fortunate brethren.[138]

The western religions all enjoin their followers to look after the poor. Even those charitable organizations which are not related to churches are composed of or supported by people whose values lead them to look outside themselves and serve the needs of others. Of course, there are mean-spirited people who never share, and some would pilfer from a collection plate passed for the poor. But virtue requires and most Americans concur that the "haves" bear a moral responsibility to see that the "have nots" obtain the basic necessities of life including food, shelter, clothing and medical care.

The Torah makes it abundantly clear that charity is expected of the Jews. In unmistakable language it says:

If, however, there is a needy person among you, one of your kinsmen in any of your settlements in the land that the Lord your God is giving you, do not harden your heart and shut your hand against your needy kinsman. Rather, you must open your hand and lend him sufficient for whatever he needs. . . . Give to him readily and have no regrets when you do so, for in return the Lord your God will bless you in all your efforts and in all your undertakings. For there will never cease to be needy ones in your land, which is why I command you: Open your

---

[138] Ibid., pp. 206-207.

hand to the poor and needy kinsman in your land.[139]

The Torah reveals a God who "upholds the cause of the fatherless and the widow, and befriends the stranger, providing him with food and clothing"[140]; and it goes on to command that, "you too must befriend the stranger, for you were strangers in the land of Egypt."[141]

We have seen that Christianity looks to charity and love for others as the commandment of God; and we see love as the method by which humankind can reflect the nature of its Creator. Paul's second epistle to the Corinthians is clear. He wrote:

> I do not mean that others should be eased and you burdened, but that as a matter of equality your abundance at the present time should supply their want, . . .[142]

and

> The point is this: he who sows sparingly will also reap sparingly, and he who sows bountifully will also reap bountifully. Each one must do as he has made up his mind, not reluctantly or under compulsion, for God loves a cheerful giver.[143]

Among the "five pillars" of the faith, Islam requires payment of the "zakat" or alms-tax which is a mandatory donation to charity, sometimes collected by the state. Thomas W. Lippman has written:

---

[139] *Torah*, Deut. 15: 7-8, 10-11.
[140] *Torah*, Deut. 10: 18.
[141] *Torah*, Deut. 10: 19.
[142] II Cor. 8: 13-14. (RSV)
[143] II Cor. 9: 6-7. (RSV)

The Koran defines the righteous as those who "attend to their prayers, pay the alms tax and firmly believe in the life to come". (31: 4) The obligation to share what one has with those less fortunate is stressed throughout the Holy Book. Islam teaches that the riches of this world are transitory and stresses that those who have abundant blessings should share with the less fortunate. The Muslim definition of the virtuous life includes charitable support of widows, wayfarers, orphans, and the poor. The zakat institutionalizes that duty. . . . Some scholars argue that the zakat should not be collected by the state, because it has spiritual merit only if voluntary.[144]

Given all of this, there should be no need for government to institute welfare programs; but it must, because too few people accept their responsibility to share. Consequently, economic issues must be resolved in a political context which is ill-suited for the purpose, and social issues are often pushed aside.

The first requirements are to identify the needy and their needs. To begin with, everybody has emotional and social needs, in addition to physical needs for food, shelter, clothing and health care. Among the emotional needs are love, self-respect and a sense of purpose in life. Among the social needs are literacy, vocational training, and a sense of responsibility for one's self and family. Any system designed to meet the needs of the poor and the helpless must balance all of these needs, and not simply draw an arbitrary "poverty line" and open the treasury doors to those who fall below it.

The next issue is related to limits of resources and their

[144] Thomas W. Lippman, *Understanding Islam* (New York: Penguin Group, Mentor, 1990), p. 18.

allocation to meet the needs which must be met by either
private charity or public welfare. The resolution of this issue carries a political sensitivity which is susceptible to emotional manipulation, as by calling one side "bleeding-heart
liberals" and the other side "mean-spirited."

All of the issues mentioned above are related to power,
and so to politics. Who shall identify the needy and their
needs? Who shall allocate the limited resources? Who shall
distribute those resources to the needy and minimize abuse
or fraud? How can that power be controlled?

Even beyond what he calls the "welfare mess,"[145] Professor Friedman lays the following premise:

> In an earlier and simpler age, a disaster such as
> Hurricane Agnes would have been met by local re-
> sources, insurance, and charitable contributions.
> Today, it is taken for granted that the federal gov-
> ernment should be the major source of emergency
> assistance and should also compensate the victims
> for the greater part of their material damage. I
> have encountered literally no questioning of this
> assumption. Yet, the change is by no means an un-
> mixed blessing.[146]

Then he goes on to say:

> . . . The real issues go deeper. What effect do these
> arrangements have on the character and efforts of
> the participants? On the use of our human and
> natural resources?
>
> One adverse effect is clear. The rest of us are en-

[145] Friedman, *No Free Lunch*, p. 207.
[146] Ibid., p. 303-304.

couraged to avoid personal involvement. We can
sympathize casually, and then go about our business. After all, Big Brother is taking care of the
victims. He is doing it with our money, so we can
feel righteous, but the connection is so remote that
we have no sense of individual participation. Surely,
nothing has done so much over the years to destroy a sense of human community, of individual
responsibility for assisting the less fortunate, as
the bureaucratizing of charity.

The victims are affected as well. Help extended to
them on a personal basis would stimulate a recip-
rocal feeling of obligation. It would strengthen their
self-reliance. Help extended by government produces resentment and weakens self-reliance. Rug-
ged individualism has been the motor of progress.
Are we sure that we have a substitute?[147]

Politicians have long since learned to hide behind a fa-
cade of euphemisms. They speak of "entitlements" so as to
conceal the stigma of reliance upon welfare; and, in so doing, they unwittingly confirm to those so inclined that "the
world owes them a living." Once "pride" or self-respect kept
people off the dole. No more. Over the last sixty years or so,
sociologists and politicians have made persistent and successful efforts to make respectable what was once not so;
and in all too many cases they have destroyed the work ethic
which was so important in America. They have created a
dependent subculture. Imagine for a moment what would
happen if we in this country:

• Face the fact that people are not equal;

---

[147] Ibid., p. 304.

- Endorse the precept that those who have more than
enough should share — either voluntarily or by taxes —
with those who are helpless because of disability, lack of
resources, or circumstances wholly beyond their control;

- Condition suffrage on self-sufficiency, or in the alternative, a sensible plan and continuing good faith effort to
achieve self-sufficiency through participation in vocational training, schooling in social responsibility, and de-
monstrable literacy in English;

- Encourage self-sufficiency by conditioning government-
funded charity on (1) helplessness plainly evidenced by
age, mental impairment or physical disability, (2) public
service by the able-bodied, and (3) demonstrated efforts
to develop the skills and attitude needed to obtain employment, even menial employment if no other be available;

- Distribute government-funded charity in a form which
cannot be converted to inappropriate or unintended use,
as by a voucher with stiff penalties for misuse by the
recipient and jail time for those who abet misuse;

- Distribution of benefits at the local level where recipi-
ents are likely to be known, with accountability to the
state level so as to minimize chances of corrupting those
directly involved in distribution; and

- Adopt federal standards of uniformity to the extent that
the states don't compete to drive out the needy into other
states with better benefits.

    If all this were to be done, the purse would not be con-
trolled by those who lay claim to the treasury through their

elected or unelected spokesmen; and politicians could not use the self-interest of the poor and ignorant for the purposes of their own election or reelection. Such a system should minimize class hatred stirred up by some so-called "advocates for the poor" and placate those who are taxed because they refuse to share.

This is not to say that the rich should not share with the poor. It is simply to say that a successful system to provide for the less fortunate must be created in a manner which is consistent with appropriate values. It should provide help for the helpless, and it should provide motivation for others to help themselves.

Of course, the intervention of a political system is necessary for the establishment and operation of either a capitalistic or a socialistic economic system. It takes government to establish and maintain the monetary system upon which either capitalism or socialism depends. Government must somehow protect the value of the medium of exchange, which is money. If people have no confidence in the medium of exchange, commerce will collapse by either horrendous inflation or catastrophic depression. Moreover, government must create and maintain a system of jurisprudence through which contracts are enforced and the economic system is harnessed to promote benefits to society as well as to the individuals who profit. The law must also protect commerce from those who would "game" the system and profit by cheating others or by manipulating the system to socially undesirable ends.

Here we come to issues of regulation. Experience clearly shows that capitalism cannot be left unregulated; for, when it is, the rich take advantage of their power to mistreat the poor and middle classes. In the United States we have learned to forbid exploitation of children by the "child labor laws"; and to require minimum wages and overtime pay by the "wage and hour laws." We use public commissions to control utilities, which by their nature must be monopolies; and our laws forbid other monopolies because of the manifest risk that they have an unfair advantage in the marketplace. Other instances of appropriate regulation include the banking, insurance and securities laws — which make an effort to inhibit harmful effects of greed in the financial sector. There are those who champion tight regulation of business, and virtually every businessman decries regulation, — especially that to which his business must conform, or which doesn't give him "an edge." We and our political leaders seem perplexed as to how much and what kind of regulation is healthy, in both the social and economic sense. According to Philip K. Howard, regulation has led to "the death of common sense," as he argues in his book with that title.[148] He says:

> We seem to have achieved the worst of both worlds: a system of regulation that goes too far while it also does too little.

> This paradox is explained by the absence of the one indispensable ingredient of any successful human endeavor: use of judgment. In the decades since World War II, we have constructed a system of regulatory law that basically outlaws common sense. . . .[149]

The solution Howard offers is that bureaucrats be given some discretion to exercise their common sense in the application of statutory and regulatory law to everyday life. He says:

---

[148] Philip K. Howard, *The Death of Common Sense* (New York: Random House, 1994).
[149] Ibid., p. 11.

It is perhaps a hateful thought to give government officials a measure of discretion, but that's the only way for them to do anything, and the only way for us to know who to blame. Giving responsibility does not imply high confidence; as New Dealer Jim Landis noted, "We must take into account that government will be operated by men of average talent and average ability." The point is to put them on the spot. . . .[150]

In a capitalistic country, taxes must be sufficient to finance the services which only government can provide. At the same time, taxes must be minimized to enlarge individual opportunity and to motivate commercial activity. It is well accepted nowadays that income tax deductions may be utilized to encourage socially beneficial conduct, while excise taxes may be used to discourage harmful conduct. So taxes serve as a control mechanism as well as revenue, and political values tend to support social values.

It is the political system through which the people make judgments necessary to determine which is beneficial to their society and which is harmful. For example, potential rewards for the risk which is necessary to energize a free enterprise system can lead some people to nonproductive speculation, through which speculators may gain or lose enormous sums of money on ventures which do not afford any social benefit, even if successful. One may argue that an individual should be left to speculate all he wants to, but where he risks the resources of others, as in corporate finance or a banking relationship, his ill-advised speculation is indefensible. It has an enormous potential for harm, to the speculator, to others, or to both. So the political system, through the force of law, asserts the necessary control to prohibit the harmful

---

[150] Ibid., pp. 180-181.

and to encourage the socially beneficial.

As we have seen, socialism requires the force of government to constantly redistribute wealth. On the other hand, free enterprise requires moral and ethical conduct. It can endure only if there are community standards of honesty, dependability, and the "sanctity" of a contract. If those standards deteriorate, the system suffers because people can no longer trust each other and an essential element of the free enterprise system is destroyed.

So one must conclude that the optimum is not socialism or "cooperative economics" as theorized by Fogler, but a system of free enterprise tempered by common sense regulation and charity — the volunteers referred to by Drucker as the "third sector." Obviously, the effort to reach and maintain equilibrium in such a free enterprise system is the cause of stress, and there never will be perfect balance of competing interests; but, stress is not necessarily unhealthy.[151] It can produce adaptation to reality.[152]

---

[151] Hans Selye, *The Stress of Life*, rev. ed. (New York: McGraw-Hill Book Co., 1978), pp. xv, 63.
[152] Ibid., p. 38.

Chapter Eight

Faith

*T*here are three worlds: The world of the child, the world of the adult, and the world of the believer.

The world of the child is a fantasy world of which he is the center around which all else revolves. He thinks the world is meant for his pleasure. He thinks people are meant to serve his needs and wishes. He expects all of his dreams to come true.

The adult thinks his is the real world. His dreams have not come true. He now knows that others will not serve all his needs and wishes. Indeed, he has been frustrated in conflicts with other people so many times that he has become cynical. Now he thinks that money buys anything and power is the goal. He sees the world in terms of the law of the jungle, where it's every man for himself and "the devil take the hindmost." Wealth, position and power are the trinity before which he genuflects. He now knows that he is not the center of the world, but he thinks that the center is populated by celebrities, the powerful, and those who are wealthier than he. He feels tan-

gential and his efforts to join himself to the inner circle so
often meet with rebuff and rejection that he is miserable.

Actually, the world of the believer is the real world. It
is the world of the spirit. Its elements cannot be weighed or
counted or measured; but, unlike the elements of the material world, they shall never pass away. The believer knows
that popularity, position, wealth and power are of no more
substance than the dreams of a child. Through faith, he has
come to realize that the center of his world is God, the ar-
chitect and builder of all. Satisfaction, joy and peace of mind
are in the third world only.

The Bible says that faith is "the assurance of things
hoped for" and "the conviction of things not seen."[153] I suspect that sounds to us more complicated than it really is.
The Bible also says that one who comes to God "must believe that He is."[154] That is a bit less difficult to understand
and simply another way of saying that you cannot have a
relationship with God if you don't believe in God.

Of course there are many people who do not believe in
God. The atheist denies the existence of God, and lives without love, forgiveness and peace. The agnostic thinks there
to be no proof of the existence of God, although he is not so
sure as to deny the "possibility." He lives in doubt and the
fear engendered by doubt. The atheist says "seeing is believing"; but the Jew, Christian and Muslim — all believers
in one God[155] — say "believing is seeing."[156] We believe, and
that belief is our nexus with the Spirit. As it is written:

God is a Spirit; and they that worship Him must
worship Him in spirit and in truth.[157]

[153] Heb. 11: 1. (NAS)
[154] Heb. 11: 6.
[155] Deut. 6: 4; Isa. 44: 6; Mark 12: 29; *The Quràn*, Surah II: 163.
[156] John 7: 17.
[157] John 4: 24.

Those of us who believe, do so without seeing God. Our belief itself is our connection with God, and it becomes the substance of our hopes and the evidence of what we cannot see. Belief develops into faith. With faith, we can confidently worship that Spirit of which there is ample evidence, but which we cannot touch or see in any physical sense. Faith links us to God.

Faith is necessary precisely because neither experience nor logic based on experience alone is sufficient to explain the spiritual. Any attempt to explain the spiritual as if it were no different from the material is foreordained to failure. Physical science may provide a partial understanding of anatomy, and scientists may have a limited comprehension of physiology; but they cannot explain *life*, much less initiate it. Living cells may replicate themselves in the laboratory, but dead cells cannot be vivified or made to reproduce by even the smartest scientist.

Who can construct an argument which will convince those humanists, who look to themselves as the product of evolution alone, that there is a "First Cause" which set the whole in motion, the Creator? Their self-centeredness blinds them to the existence of a Power greater than themselves, to a Purpose which they haven't defined, and to a Promise of life beyond that which they can see. They deprive themselves of the Peace which comes to those who truly believe.

What is their reason for denying that they were created and that their very life itself depends on the Creator? Do they think the teachings of the Torah or the Gospel or the Quràn are evil? Do Jesus' teachings of love offend them? If we accept their denials, where are we led? To a better life? Maybe God didn't do things the way the humanists would have done them; but don't you disbelieve on that account.

Do you believe in life? Can you see life? Oh, you can see evidence of life in yourself, in others, and in animals and plants. But you can't see life itself. Do you believe in love?

Love can't be counted or measured or weighed.

If you believe there is life — which itself cannot be seen, and if you believe there is love — which can't be counted, measured or weighed, then you believe that existence of the spiritual is perceived by physical evidence. To argue otherwise, i.e., that the spiritual cannot exist without itself being observed is to argue backward from a conclusion reached beforehand. Such an argument is not reason, but obstinate blindness to reality. And who is blinder than he who refuses to see?

There are many things we don't understand, but believe. "Rationalism" is our inheritance from the Age of Enlightenment, which hitched science to rebellion against the Roman Church leaders who were arrogant and corrupt. But corruption of churchmen doesn't disprove the truth of the gospel message; it only proves that power can corrupt even popes and kings. Consider these questions, and think on them:

- Were the truths "proven" by science true before science said so?

- Are there truths today which have yet to be discovered by scientists?

- May there be truths which will never be demonstrated by scientific methods?

- If so, must we ignore all evidence of such truths just because science hasn't "proven" them, and may never do so?

- May we not then look beyond science and act upon evidence of spiritual truths which do not admit of scientific proof?

With all its successful use, and indeed it has had much in the material world, the scientific method cannot be used to examine peace of mind or love. It just doesn't work in the realm of the spirit. At best, science explains only "what" and "how," and even those imperfectly. It cannot explain "why" and "by whom." Science depends upon statistical analysis; and the truth of God cannot be counted, measured or weighed. So while science can explain some of the material, that fact does not exclude the spiritual.

Our faith is not senseless. It is grounded in reason. "Rational faith" is not an oxymoron. Reason leads us to faith. Reason tells us that the heavens and the earth, with all of their complexities which scientists cannot resolve or understand or explain, cannot have "just happened." What we see persuades us that there are things unseen. Just a look around us, at the awesome complexity of the material, compels a belief in the spiritual.[158] Nothing so intricate, complicated, involved and elaborate as human anatomy and physiology could be other than designed. We call the designer God. And it doesn't matter whether Creation took six days or six million years. The point is: some incomparable spiritual power caused and created the heavens and the earth; and we call that spirit God. I cannot explain God. Nor do I need to. By His grace, my faith is sufficient to establish my relationship to Him.[159]

Why do we try to relate to God?

First, all of us soon learn that we cannot depend wholly upon ourselves. We must look outside ourselves for even life itself. From the earliest times and in every tribe and culture there has been a search by men and women for something apart from themselves upon which they could depend. Some worshipped the sun, which brought them warmth and light. Some worshiped the earth, out of which grew their food. Some created idols in their own image or in the image

[158] See Rom. 1: 20.
[159] See Luke 10: 21; Eph. 2: 8; I Cor. 2: 1-5.

of beasts. In each case, they were looking outside themselves for something upon which they could depend. Those who believe in God depend on God, the Creator himself, not some thing which either He or they themselves have created. By faith we believe that He who gives us life and sustains it day by day is dependable.

Secondly, we need God in order to focus our attention outside ourselves. Self-centered people are painfully unhappy because they can never get enough attention. The world simply refuses to revolve around them. They come up empty in every relationship, feeling that nobody loves them as much as they deserve. They are always in a state of anxiety. They cannot find peace of mind. It is only to the extent that we direct our attention outwardly that we find peace; and it is our belief in God which brings us to that.

We need God to show us purpose and meaning in life. Any of us who believes in God as the creator and source of life must agree, on that ground alone, that our lives have purpose in God's system of things. Otherwise creation would be vain and meaningless, aimless and signifying nothing. We need God to reveal to us His purpose and meaning for our lives. We need His spirit to connect with our longings and to give us light to find His way.

Some may differ, and do; but I believe that each of us may choose whether to seek and to serve God's purpose for his life, or not. In his recent book, Pope John Paul II makes a strikingly awesome statement:

> God created man as rational and free, thereby placing Himself under man's judgment.[160]

If one chooses to accept God's sovereignty in his life, and to serve God's purpose by his life, he thereby puts him-

---

[160] John Paul II, *Crossing the Threshold of Hope*, p. 61.

self in synch with God. In no other way can he come to know peace of mind. And if one chooses to reject God, who loses? God? No way! He was in the beginning, and evermore shall be. If you reject Him, you reject purpose and power, light and love, even everlasting life.

God's purpose for some is the ministry; but not for all. There is purpose in lay service, in and outside the church, in medicine and law and business and in all the other good and decent vocations in which people serve the needs of others.[161]

To identify God's purpose for your own life, first inventory your talents. Surely they provide a clue. Then look for opportunities to develop and use those talents — being sure to measure those opportunities by your yardstick of values. Finally, pray for guidance and it will come.

I believe in Jesus; and you may well ask "Why?" Each of us must answer that question for himself; but as for me, I have come to believe that the resurrection of Jesus is an historical fact.

The Jews of Jesus' day wanted a sign,[162] and the Greeks wanted to argue philosophy.[163] But Jesus said, "Blessed are those who have not seen and yet believe."[164] And Paul warned the Romans against "disputes over opinions."[165]

Even philosophers and theologians must depend on faith for truth. If they rely on reason alone, they stumble because the spirit does not surrender to reason. That is why Professor Crossan must develop his own definitions and premises, denying even the possibility of Jesus' miracles, in order to "prove" that He was only human.[166] That author claims ad-

---

[161] See Rom. 12: 4-8.
[162] Matt. 12: 38; 16: 1; Mark 8: 11; Luke 11: 16.
[163] Acts 17: 16-21.
[164] John 20: 29. (RSV)
[165] Rom. 14: 1. (RSV)
[166] John Dominic Crossan, *Jesus, A Revolutionary Biography* (San Francisco: Harper, 1994).

herence to a "methodological process," saying:

> My method locates the historical Jesus where three
> independent vectors (cross cultural anthropology,
> Greco-Roman and Jewish history, and the gospels
> — both canonical and apocryphal) cross. That tri-
> angulation serves as internal discipline and mu-
> tual corrective, since *all* must intersect at the same
> point for *any* of them to be correct.[167]

In spite of those "good intentions", Professor Crossan's
conclusions find only the canon to be in error. His bias is
evident. He says that "miracles are not changes in the physical world so much as changes in the social world."[168] He
does not believe in "supernatural spirits who invade our
bodies from outside"[169] so he cannot accept exorcism. He
says, "I do not think that anyone, anywhere, at any time
brings dead people back to life."[170] So, in spite of his protes-
tations of fairness, he must construct elaborate schemes to
explain away the raising of Lazarus and the resurrection of
Jesus. His arguments beg the questions, referring to the
gospels as "mythology,"[171] "Lukan propaganda,"[172] and "fiction"[173]. He speaks this way of the gospels even while describing his own conclusions as "my interpretation,"[174] "sheer
speculation,"[175] "my suspicion,"[176] and "I can imagine"[177] and

---

[167] Ibid., p. xi; parenthetical explanation and emphasis added.
[168] Ibid., p. 82.
[169] Ibid., p. 85.
[170] Ibid., p. 95; and see pp. 158, 161.
[171] Ibid., pp. 18, 26.
[172] Ibid., p. 26.
[173] Ibid., p. 35.
[174] Ibid., p. 78.
[175] Ibid., p. 24.
[176] Ibid., p. 43.
[177] Ibid., p. 47.

he tends to give far more credibility to apocrypha and to 20th century writers than to the canonical books.

Ask yourself this question: Did these "peasants," as Crossan calls them, and Galilean fishermen so hoodwink the world for two thousand years that it takes Professor Crossan to open our eyes with his self-described speculation?

In our time, the iconoclastic intellectual elite replace the pharisaical elite and, because Jesus threatens the basis of their social standing, they deny Him. They *must* deny him; because to believe something they cannot understand strikes at the very intellectualism which they worship. This is why they create controversies where none before existed, and resolve every controverted issue against the faith.

Who can produce a sign which some people won't doubt? Roman soldiers, who were professionals at crucifixion, assured Pilate that Jesus was dead[178], and He was buried in a new tomb, sealed with a large rock.[179] Pilate sent soldiers to guard the tomb.[180] Yet on the third day He arose, and was seen by many of His followers during the next 40 days. Those who claimed to be eyewitnesses[181] to His appearances after the Resurrection gave their lives rather than recant.[182] According to the Roman historian, Tacitus, the Christians were truly martyrs. He said:

> They were put to death with exquisite cruelty, and to their sufferings Nero added mockery and derision. Some were covered with the skins of wild beasts and left to be devoured by dogs; others were nailed to crosses; numbers were burnt alive; and

[178] John 19: 33; Mark 15: 42-45.
[179] Matt. 27: 60; Mark 15: 46.
[180] Matt. 27: 62-66.
[181] II Pet. 1: 16-18; I John 1: 1-3.
[182] William Alva Gifford, *The Story of the Faith* (New York: The MacMillan Company, 1946), pp. 118-119.

many, covered over with inflammable matter, were lighted up when the day declined, to serve as torches during the night.[183]

These were good men; men who taught truth and virtue; men who warned of Hell, and held out the hope of Heaven to those who believe. They were not the sort of men who could have conspired to perpetrate a fraud on their friends and families, — especially knowing the penalties visited upon believers by the authorities, both Roman and Jewish.

I cannot believe their story of the Resurrection to be a cleverly devised fable. Galilean fishermen of that day, whom Crossen refers to as "peasants", could not have made up such a story. Nor did they have a motive for lying. All they gained from their testimony was ridicule, poverty, stripes, earthly dishonor, disgrace and ultimately death; — unless their testimony *was* true and their Lord *had* risen.

We need not look to the gospels alone for evidence that the early Christians believed their Lord to have risen from the dead. Flavius Josephus, a Judean of noble birth who became a protege of the Roman Emperor Vespasian, included in his extensive work what has come to be known as the "Testimonium Flavianum." Josephus was a contemporary of the Apostle Paul. Indeed, he first travelled to Rome only three or four years after Paul did so. A critical biography of this Jewish historian was first published in France in 1989 and then translated into English.[184] The author says:

[183] Tacitus, *Annals XV*, xxxiii-xliv, as quoted in Gifford, ibid., p. 118.
[184] Mireille Hadas-Level, *Flavius Josephus, Eyewitness to Rome's First-Century Conquest of Judea*, Translation by Richard Miller (New York: Macmillan Publishing Company, 1993).

So integral is this writer to the history of Christianity that the relative obscurity into which Josephus has
lapsed in our own century can be viewed as another
clear sign of the de-Christianization of the West.[185]

She also writes that:

Without his testimony we would know nothing of
the history of Judea between 100 B.C.E. and year
74 of our era apart from a few fragmentary words
from the pens of Greek or Latin authors or the
semilegendary tales of the Talmud . . .[186]

In *Antiquities of the Jews*, Josephus included the
Testimonium Flavianum in the following language, as translated by William Whiston:

Now, there was about this time, Jesus, a wise man,
if it be lawful to call him a man, for he was a doer
of wonderful works, — a teacher of such men as receive the truth with pleasure. He drew over to him
both many of the Jews, and many of the Gentiles.
He was [the] Christ; and when Pilate, at the suggestion of the principal men amongst us, had condemned
him to the cross, those that loved him at the first did
not forsake him, for he appeared to them alive again
the third day, as the divine prophets had foretold
these and ten thousand other wonderful things concerning him; and the tribe of Christians, so named
from him, are not extinct at this day.[187]

---

[185] Ibid., p. 229.
[186] Ibid., p. 3
[187] Flavius Josephus, *Antiquities of the Jews*, Book XVIII, Chapter III,
paragraph 3, Translation by William Whiston (Grand Rapids, MI:
Kregel Publications, 1981), p. 379.

Crossan says "some later Christian editor delicately Christianized his account"[188] and there have been those who express doubt that the Testimonium Flavianum was actually written by Josephus; but the work went unquestioned for 1500 years.[189]

With all this evidence, it seems only reasonable to believe that those who professed to have seen Jesus risen from the dead told the truth. Unlike the disciples and those early Christians, I have never seen a physical manifestation of Christ. But I believe, and my belief links me to Jesus as to God. The Catholic Archbishop of New York, John Cardinal O'Connor, recently put it this way:

> I don't see how, without the gift of faith, you would believe he (Jesus) was the Son of God. Faith makes the difference. You can study the Scriptures till your eyes fall out, and without the gift of faith, you're not going to believe Christ was the Son of God. The miracle is faith itself.[190]

So Jesus' revelation of His Father identifies God for all believers as our Father, too. Through Jesus we can see the nature and character of God. Every single thing which Jesus taught was good. Anyone who has ever truly tried to follow Jesus has been a better person for it.

Jews and Muslims treat Jesus as a prophet, but deny His divinity because there is only one God. Christians are also monotheists,[191] but believe that one God can be per-

---

[188] Crossan, *Jesus Biography*, p. 162.
[189] Hadas-Lebel, *Flavius Josephus, Eyewitness*, p. 226.
[190] John Cardinal O'Connor, Archbishop of New York, quoted in "Who Was Jesus?" *Life Magazine*, December, 1994, p. 71.
[191] John 10: 30; I Tim. 2: 5.

ceived in any of three forms: Father, Son and Holy Spirit. One chemical compound, H_20, can be perceived as water, ice or steam.

We all know that there are people who deny that Jesus ever lived, and some who deny the existence of God Himself. They argue long and hard for their position, and scoff at us who profess faith. Before spending much of your time listening to their arguments, ask them to explain how unbelief makes life better — for themselves, for others, or for the world.

Why believe the Bible? My own experience leads me to believe that "the way" which is described and taught by the Bible is the way to peace of mind in relationships with both God and men. It appears to me to teach truth; and, indeed, that "the truth will make you free."[192] While it teaches liberty[193], the Bible also warns that liberty must not be misused.[194] Its directions for a good and wholesome life are explicit and plainly best for both the individual and the community.[195]

With faith, you can use prayer to reach the ear of God, to speak to Him and then listen to His voice within you. Prayer need not be a formal, structured experience; it need only be a sincere voice addressed to God. Your prayers may include professions of faith and worship, and acknowledgments of awe at the wonders of creation. They should express thanksgiving — both in general terms and for specific blessings. You may intercede with God by prayer for others. Then, as to yourself, your prayers should be for forgiveness, guidance and strength. Don't forget to pray.[196]

[192] John 8: 32. (RSV)
[193] I Cor. 6: 12; 10: 23.
[194] Gal. 5: 13-14.
[195] cf. Phil. 4: 8.
[196] Luke 18: 1.

Whose hands has God on Earth to serve, — but ours?
Whose feet has God on Earth to send, — but ours?
Oh, how we pray for Him to help,
and hope for Him to intervene!
His miracles He works by using us,
If we but lend our hands and feet to Him.

One cannot rise from prayer and walk away expecting the heavens to open and angels to descend for action in response to prayer. Old-timers say "put feet to your faith". This means that one should act in accordance with his prayers; himself doing his part to bring about their answer.

But I cannot write a theology textbook for you. It is in church, in Bible study, and in your own seeking that you will come to a stronger faith and find the light to guide your own life. If you seek, you will find: — faith and love and peace.[197]

J. B. Philips challenges us with this thought:

Suppose Christianity is not a *religion* at all but a way of life . . .[198]

Whatever the circumstances in which you live, your life will be affected by your beliefs. In a sense, you will become what you believe. Your choices will mirror your beliefs. If you have the faith which links your life with God, your thought processes will be affected, your behavior will be affected, your relationships with other people will be affected, and you will come to experience the peace of mind which "passeth all understanding."[199]

---

[197] Matt. 7: 7; Luke 11: 9.
[198] J. B. Philips, *When God Was Man* (New York: Abingdon Press, 1955), p. 38.
[199] Phil. 4: 7.

So, believe — and live by your belief. But do so in the spirit of love and humility, not in the spirit of pride. Although some of our beliefs of themselves exclude the contrary, in the same way as the truth excludes error, bear always in mind that arrogance in belief has led the world to war again and again and again. Arrogance, even in the belief for which one is willing to give his life, is a species of pride. It excludes love, and it substitutes intolerance for those whose relationship to the same God is on a different plane.[200]

Finally, it is faith that gives us hope. Hope as well as faith is to be drawn from the Resurrection of Jesus Christ. While it appears for a time that evil conquers and death prevails, we Christians can look to Jesus in hope and faith that death is not the end, and that good will ultimately triumph over evil.[201]

---

[200] Rom. 14: 2-6; 11-17.
[201] Rom. 8: 24-25.

Chapter Nine

Love: What is it? How Do You Give It? and How Do You Get It?

*E*verybody wants to be loved.
Perhaps nothing is more important to us than love. Yet it is misunderstood, abused, manipulated, and treated flippantly so often as to make us shake our heads in wonderment. Everybody talks about love, — sometimes seriously and sometimes foolishly. What is sometimes said makes us wonder if some people have even the vaguest notion of what love means.

The Bible says that God is love.[202] Its injunctions include: Love God.[203] Love your neighbor.[204] Love your enemies.[205] Love your family.[206] Indeed, the Master said: "A new commandment I give unto you, that ye love one another."[207]

---

[202] I John 4: 8, 16.
[203] Josh. 23: 11; Matt. 22: 37.
[204] Lev. 19: 18; Matt. 22: 39.
[205] Matt. 5: 44.
[206] Exod. 20: 12; Eph. 5: 25; Titus 2: 4.
[207] John 13: 34.

So, what is love? It cannot be the same in all instances; that is, to love husbands or wives cannot be the same as to love neighbors. To love one's children cannot be the same as to love one's enemies. My suggestion to you is that love be defined in the abstract and that the definition be studied then in specific circumstances. I shall try to help you see how this can be done.

First, I suggest that, in the simplest form, love means a solicitous concern which leads one to focus on others and to serve their needs. This is a bare bones definition, and in the context of specific circumstances, love may have additional elements. As we ponder on the nature of love in the context of specific circumstances in which we express love, we must think about (1) our relationships, (2) our resources, and (3) our responsibilities. Bear those in mind as you read on.

The first and greatest commandment is to "love the Lord your God with all your heart and with all your soul and with all your mind."[208] There are no conditions. This commandment is an absolute. In the shortest and simplest terms it calls for us to seek the will and purpose of God for our lives and to serve His will and purpose, whatever it may be and at whatever "cost" to us. Our relationship to God must be the first and foremost of all of our priorities, including relationships with others.[209] Our resources must not get in the way.[210] The commandment itself makes it clear that we have no responsibilities with a priority greater than that of loving God.

Love of God is expressed by thanksgiving, praise and worship; but, that's not all. Jesus told his disciples, "If ye love me, keep my commandments."[211] Moreover, love of God

---

[208] Matt. 22: 37-38. (NAS)
[209] Matt. 10: 37; 12: 46-50.
[210] Matt. 16: 24-26.
[211] John 14: 15; and see John 14: 21, 23-24.

is also expressed in the active love of other people.[212] Jesus repeatedly told Peter that his love would require that he "feed My sheep."[213]

That brings us to the second commandment: "You shall love your neighbor as yourself."[214] Jesus was asked the same question which jumps to our minds, "who is my neighbor?" In reply, He told the story of a good Samaritan. The Jews and the Samaritans hated each other, much as the Jews and the Palestinians do today. Yet this Samaritan went out of his way to meet the needs of a Jew who had been beaten and left for dead by robbers. We are told to "do likewise."[215] This is love in its simplest form, in its fundamental or elementary sense. It proceeds from a kind heart, and it is what we often call charity. It is love without a relationship. This love shows itself in courtesy, civility and the graciousness of one who is considerate of other people. It serves others' needs; but it likewise serves a need of our own — a need to be useful. Do you ever feel lonely? Try love. It will take your mind off yourself, make you feel needed, and warm up your spirit. We can feel good, even about sharing our resources with others, and be concerned only with the limit set by our other responsibilities, such as family.

The injunction to "love your enemies"[216] is a tough one. How can we love those who are out to destroy us? As our example, Jesus prayed for His enemies; asking that they be forgiven. And He did so even as they crucified Him.[217] I can only tell you that you *can* have a solicitous concern for people whom you don't respect; you *can* focus on the needs of people for whom you have no affection; you can even meet the needs

---

[212] Matt. 7: 12; 18-27; 25: 31-46.
[213] John 21: 15-17.
[214] Matt. 22: 39. (NAS)
[215] Luke 10: 25-37.
[216] Matt. 5: 44.
[217] Luke 23: 34.

of people who show no appreciation or gratitude. If you do these things, you will have a greater respect for yourself in the knowledge that you have done what is right. Anger and hate turn on the wrong "juices" inside us, and do more harm to us than to the objects of our anger and hate. Instead of letting your emotions boil over with anger and hate, you will feel emotions of peace and satisfaction. Unless you let these emotions turn into self-righteousness, as some people seem to do, you will feel warmth and security.

As children, love your parents. Your relationship with them is one which parallels your relationship with God, who is our heavenly Father. Here, between children and parents, love also includes affection and respect. Youngsters do not focus on financial resources; but your time and attention and hugs and helpfulness are resources which you may use to express love to your parents. Obedience and good behavior also show love toward your parents. None of these intrude upon your responsibilities to other people. Adult children are sometimes called upon to expend financial resources for the benefit of their parents. Some do so in a kind of "pay back" for the resources utilized by their parents in caring for them when they were helpless children. In using their financial resources for their parents, adult children must take into consideration the responsibilities they have for others, including their own children. Resources are usually limited, so they must be fairly and appropriately allocated, depending upon the needs of each and also upon the availability of other sources of assistance.

Romantic love includes the elements of solicitous concern, affection and respect about which we have spoken, but it also includes a chemical element related to the hormonal activities of the male and the female. This chemical complication can produce either good or bad results, depending in great measure upon the people involved. Puppy love, the courting experience, and marriage lead to the establishment of a new family with all of the good and worthwhile effects the formation of a family can bring. On the other hand, premarital sex, unwed pregnancies, sexually transmitted diseases, and adultery are some of the tragic and heartbreaking results of the distortion of love by chemistry, and the wrong choices made in the name of love. The risks in romantic love are enormous. They call for a clearheaded focus on your relationship, resources, and responsibilities to other people, sometimes other people yet unborn.

Romantic love need not end when a marital relationship is established. Indeed, both partners hope and believe that it will always endure. Love changes as the people grow. If they are wise, they find ways in which they grow together and not apart. Everybody needs a best friend, a confidant, a sidekick. Even the Lone Ranger had Tonto. The marital relationship affords the opportunity for the deepest kind of companionship. The best marriages are when husband and wife are best friends. This requires each of them to focus on the needs of the other and to use their own resources to meet those needs. Those resources include time, attention, and hugs, as well as financial support. As they share experiences with each other, they are drawn closer and their love grows stronger. But for such a wonderful relationship, the couple must have prepared well for marriage. Even while in the throes of romantic love they must have chosen well their respective spouses. Chemistry may be an indicator of a good marital relationship, but it is by no means the only factor to be considered. A couple's chances of a successful marriage are immeasurably increased if they come from the same cultural background, if they share interests which will survive the wedding itself, and if they are maturing and becoming less and less self-centered.

Out of the marriage comes the child. What parents believe to be love sometimes has elements of a possessory interest or even self-centeredness. That is not truly love, and parents should take pains to avoid treating their children as only extensions of themselves. While the affection for a youngster may arise from its cute and lovable behavior as a baby, love requires that it have the respect due any other individual. Parental love is love of a high order because the relationship is one of dependency from the outset. Priorities shift when children are added to a family, and responsibility to others is necessarily secondary to the responsibility to one's children. Resources available to the family must be utilized for the benefit of young children, before there is a legitimate claim on the part of others. Moreover, parental love brings forth care, nurture and education of the child; so the parents have the foremost responsibility of inculcating in their children the cultural standards of morals and ethics to which they themselves are heirs. Throughout this experience, the family members can be drawn closer to each other by shared experiences which become tradition, such as those of Thanksgiving and Christmas for example.

Some of the elements of love as I have described it are common to nature and not exclusively human. For example, many of the animals manifest an affection and regard for their offspring which cannot be well called anything other than love. They focus on the needs of their young and use their own resources to meet those needs. But of mankind even more is required. *We* are to love one another, to love our neighbors, and even to love our enemies.

So you may ask: "What are the signs of love? How may I know it when I see it?" I would be foolish and presumptuous to answer such questions without referring you to "the love chapter" of the Bible.[218] It tells us of the signs of love, namely: patience, kindness, generosity, humility, courtesy, unselfishness, good temper, guilelessness and sincerity. Note that it speaks less of an emotion than of an attitude. It is

---

[218] I Cor. 13.

not so much a response to someone else as a spirit inside oneself. It does not require reciprocity, but giving. Giving even as little as a sincere compliment or a word of praise is giving; and unspoken praise is the loss of an opportunity to express love. You can love those who don't love you first, and even those who don't love you at all. You yourself are in control, and experience teaches that most of those who are loved respond in kind; — not all, but so many as to make outgoing love usually attract incoming love.

Heed these words of warning. Rejection of another's love is difficult; and when one is offered unwanted romantic love, he must be very careful to decline in a loving spirit and so avoid as much as possible any hurt, even though creation of a romantic relationship would be unwise. Manipulation of another's love for you is not love; it is reprehensible. Taking advantage of love is not worthy of you; and, to the contrary, it marks a lack of love.

Sometimes we hear love referred to as "unconditional love" or "non-judgmental love." Those two adjectives are different. Their subtle difference should be understood.

"Unconditional love" is love without any requirement or prerequisite. It is not self-seeking or demanding. It is freely given. By its very nature, real love is unconditional. To place conditions on love is a contradiction. To do so is manipulative, and requires control as the price of "love." Real love cannot be bought or sold. It can only be given.

"Non-judgmental love" is love of a person whose beliefs and behavior are different from your own. It does not require acceptance of his beliefs and behavior, but only a willingness to serve his needs out of a solicitous concern.

Maybe the most difficult part of love is trying to understand why the people we love do things they shouldn't, say things they shouldn't, and act like they shouldn't. Why do our parents and children and our spouses do things which hurt and disappoint us? Sometimes the problem is ourselves.

Sometimes we don't see their point of view because we are too self-centered. Maybe we should back off a minute and try to see the other side. Children, your parents surely love you. Maybe they are trying to save you from a painful mistake when you think they are "just yelling" at you. Parents, your children surely love you. Maybe they are trying to get attention when they do something which looks stupid to you. Husbands and wives, bite your tongues and try to realize what a difficult day your spouse has had. All of us must remember that love requires patience.

We first saw that we are governed by law and ethics and moral standards. These provide rules for our behavior toward one another. Now we see that there is an even higher standard, that of love.

When love is the motive and the measure, there are no "loopholes" in the law. The moral imperative of love does not permit the use of one's imagination to find ways to evade the spirit of the law by strained interpretations of its letter. So Paul wrote:

> Love does no wrong to a neighbor; love therefore is the fulfillment of the law.[219]

———————

[219] Rom. 13: 10. (NAS)

Chapter Ten

Culture, Subcultures and Countercultures

*M*y dictionary defines "culture" as "the totality of socially transmitted behavior patterns, arts, beliefs, institutions, and all other products of human work and thought characteristic of a community or population."[220] That is a comprehensive definition. For our purposes here, I will try to simplify it somewhat and refer only to the system of values and behavior patterns which grandfathers think of as being "the American way," which we inherited from our own parents and much of which traces back to the earliest days of our country. These are the beliefs and behavior patterns which we should transmit to the generations which follow us.

An understanding of our "culture" and "the American way" must take into account the origin of cultures, the prevalence of subcultures, the dangers of counter-cultures, and the difficulties in absorbing into the national community those who

[220] *The American Heritage Dictionary.*

come from and cling to different cultural backgrounds. First, one must understand that the origin of culture is in family, tribe and community. It is expressed through language and/or dialect, religion, food, dress, and etiquette or "manners."

Out of this origin and these elements comes a system of values, including those related to behavior. Cultural differences exist because of different tribal, ethnic, and national backgrounds. Cultures also differ between social and economic classes; as well as between people from small towns and those from cities, or mountain folk and those from the "flatlands."

It is not so easy as one might suppose to cross over from one culture to another. Indeed, we speak of "culture shock" in traveling to other areas or countries which have cultures substantially different from our own. To live in another culture can create overwhelming economic and social concerns. For all but the strongest of people, there is insecurity, self-consciousness, discomfort, and even anxiety. Adaptation to a "foreign" culture can be difficult, but the alternative to adaptation can be worse. Ghettos or enclaves of immigrants provide comfort for the first generation, but they are counterproductive to assimilation of their children into the predominant culture of the nation into which the parents have immigrated. Failure to enter into the predominant culture creates disadvantages in many ways, including a lack of access to economic and social resources of the "new home." This can lead to embarrassment and timidity. Contrariwise, it can lead to belligerence. It expresses itself in both actions and attitudes. From those in the predominant culture, newcomers are often met with resentment. All too often, they do not resist temptation to take advantage of the newcomers' lack of familiarity with the predominant culture. As a famous basketball coach sarcastically complained of his team's visit to New York City, "we were strangers and 'they took us in.'"

These difficulties tend to preserve cultural differences in subcultures, which perforce inhibit the spirit of community. The problems can be alleviated if the newcomers learn by imitation, take training in the language and skills of their new home, and help each other cope with their problems of assimilation. Those of the predominant culture owe the newcomers both compassion and outreach. This is true everywhere, but especially so in America, which takes pride in a history of acceptance of those from other lands and cultures.

Newcomers to this country have chosen to immigrate because of the special nature of "the American way." Given that fact, it seems not inappropriate to insist that "the American way" remain the predominant culture and that others strive for assimilation, especially in the acceptance of values upon which this country has been established and upon which it rests.

The foundation of "the American way" is the family, primary and ultimate responsibility to and for which each person should assume. Its framework is of political and economic systems which offer freedom from the inherited classes culture and, with that, the opportunity for each individual to make a better life for himself and his family through dedication and hard work. Its structure is bound together by patriotism, well-expressed in the pledge which should be repeatedly made as a sort of national "mission statement":

> I pledge allegiance to the flag of the United States of America and to the republic for which it stands; one nation, under God, indivisible, with liberty and justice for all.

This system of values is unique in the world. While much of it was transmitted to this country from northern Europe, other parts came from the Mediterranean countries. Its basic moral premises are drawn from a Judeo-Christian background and were frankly related to religion from the beginning. Thus the motto on our coins and currency: "In God we trust."

Our heritage of freedom and the opportunities America offers us we sometimes take for granted; but these were defined and won for us by those who went before us and now fill graves from Jamestown to Arlington and from the frontiers of Kentucky to the rocky coasts of California. They brought to this country the Rule of Law, without which freedom cannot exist, and they fashioned a constitutional government with limited powers. They conquered the wilderness, cleared the farmlands, and built our cities and towns. They provided us with "the American way."

In recent years, "the American way" has been ridiculed by some who use its most precious principles to mount their attack. For example, the entertainment industry, especially television, has held the American family and its values up to ridicule. It first portrayed the father as an autocrat or a fool, and the mother as the only source of wisdom and understanding. When that became "old hat" it portrayed the children as the only source of intelligence in the American family, although they were subjected week after week to bumbling parents who misunderstood them and their peers. Having been subjected to endless hours of this garbage from the time they could first sit up to watch television, it is little wonder that children of the last thirty years show precious little respect for their parents or other adults.

Elsewhere I shall deal with "cultural literacy" and the essential nature of background cultural information to understanding what one hears and reads. Of course I cannot in this message to you exhaust the whole of "the American way," even though most of what I share with you in this book are its elements. I must emphasize for you that it has brought this country to the place where it is the envy of the world. Every day people from other countries risk their lives to immigrate, legally or illegally, into the United States. Its political and economic systems have produced what is arguably the greatest nation ever in the history of the world. Although dissidents have utilized their right to free speech for the purpose of incessantly criticizing the United States, few of them have gone elsewhere to find a better life. Currently, there is a difference of opinion as to whether the American culture has benefited from its religious traditions and the moral values drawn from them. I take the affirmative position in that debate because I believe the wholesome traits of honesty, courage, responsibility, justice, charity and obedience to lawful authority are values derived from religion and, as I have said, our Judeo-Christian heritage. But my views may conflict with what you see on television, read in your newspapers, and hear from modern educators. For that reason, to live by the principles here expressed may be for you like swimming upstream. It will take courage on your part, but it will be well worth it. I think you will not be alone, because I think that there are millions of people in this country who share the cultural values which I am trying to pass on to you.

There are also countercultures out there. They are not just perennial rebellions of the young and insecure. Some are championed by so-called "liberal" people who find traditional values too restrictive for their tastes and scoff at many things which others of us hold dear. Their principal tools are the media, the entertainment industry and the public schools. Their principal thesis is "if it feels good, do it." They shirk responsibility and find some way to blame the consequences of their influence and actions on somebody else. They seek their own interests even if harm is done to others. In my lifetime, they have brought many of our fellow citizens to prefer the quick and easy way, to search for entertainment rather than enlightenment, to grow self-centered in the name of constitutional rights, and to prefer government-provided security instead of the freedom to achieve. Much of this has been done in the name of "diversity" and upon the premise that young people suffer the loss of self-esteem if they are criticized. In order that there will be no ground for criticism, we are told that any culture is as good as any other culture, so any cultural value is as good as any other cultural value. According to them, in a democracy blessed with diversity, everybody is equal so everything is tolerated. This is pure nonsense, but it is accepted by those who find it easier to do what *feels* good than to do what *is* good. Allan Bloom has expressed the truth in this fashion:

> . . . the fact that there have been different opinions about good and bad in different times and places in no way proves that none is true or superior to others. To say that it does so prove is as absurd as to say that the diversity of points of view expressed in a college bull session proves there is no truth.[221]

Much of today's inner-city counterculture can be traced to these influences. Values once taught by families in the cities, even in poverty-stricken neighborhoods, cannot now be taught by families because in many cases there are no families. The family relationship has been destroyed by a combination of self-centered infidelity and government welfare programs. Teenaged mothers who themselves were born to teenaged mothers, with the fathers in both generations having neither lived with nor provided for the children, cannot have learned moral and ethical values in the home. Thirty years of value-neutral teaching in the public schools has not been supportive of family values, even for those children who come from stable homes. So all too many of them grow up in the streets and accept without question the coun-

---

[221] Allan Bloom, *Closing of the American Mind*, p. 39.

terculture of the streets.

Notice, now, that my criticism is not directed at color, but at the *counterculture*. Behavior which is now tolerated in the inner cities is wholly unacceptable to most black people. Those in "the older generation" deplore it. Counterculture and behavior are matters of choice. Simply being born black is not. The problem is not color; but culture, — counterculture. In the larger black community are men and women of great character and patience who share a deep religious faith. Their spokesmen describe the elements of this counterculture and make eloquent pleas for change.

William Raspberry, an African-American syndicated columnist in the Washington Post Writers Group recently wrote:

> . . . our young people are learning to disregard . . . the manners their elders have taught them.
>
> Take something as simple as dress. The lesson of the elders, who grew up believing that "clothes make the man," is that young people should dress in such a way as to distinguish themselves from their trouble-prone peers. The lesson young people are absorbing these days is that their survival may depend on dressing — and speaking and swaggering — like what the old folk used to call the "bad element."
>
> . . . the styles are copied from the "bad element" — and for good reason. Wearing the wrong clothes can get you hurt.[222]

---

[222] William Raspberry, Washington Post Writers Group, *Lexington* (KY) *Herald-Leader*, Nov. 18, 1994.

Even earlier, Raspberry analyzed this problem when he discussed an essay by Elijah Anderson, saying:

> Anderson's analysis hangs on what he sees as the two main and competing orientations of inner-city life: the "decent people" and "street people". The former tend to embrace mainstream values, attend church, work hard, negotiate their way out of conflict and sacrifice for their children, whose lives they expect will be better than their own. The latter are likelier to be ineffectual or inconsistent parents, have severely restricted financial resources, live lives characterized by disorganization and adhere to a code that explicitly accepts violence as a way of earning and maintaining respect — an exaggerated sense of manhood.
>
> . . . Its self-image has little to do with intellectual accomplishment and everything to do with being someone not to mess with.[223]

Dr. Martin Luther King spoke of having a dream about his children one day living "in a land where they will not be judged by the color of their skin, but by the content of their character." All too many people have truncated his statement to emphasize Dr. King's hope that color would be not the measure; and they have ignored his assumption that character is a proper basis for judgment. It is not wrong to express concern about the character inculcated by a culture, counterculture, or subculture. Indeed, a community cannot survive unless it manifests concern about the character of its people. King's name should never be invoked to condone

---

[223] William Raspberry, Washington Post Writers Group, *Lexington* (KY) *Herald-Leader*, May 3, 1994.

a counterculture which is destructive of character.
Another African-American syndicated columnist with
the Washington Post Writers Group is Donna Britt. She
speaks of this counterculture as "look at me-itis," relates it
to showboating in football and basketball, calls it "a cul-
ture-wide thing," and goes on to say:

> Where "look at me" is primarily, and tragically, a
> black thing is on city streets, where in-your-face
> too often results in in-your-grave. Every black adult
> in the nation needs to be pulling some kid's coat-
> tail, screaming that life, not some boneheaded no-
> tion of manhood, is worth fighting for.
>
> . . . And unless all of America rediscovers restraint as
> an art form, millions more will discover what too
> many hard young brothers "find" after their refusal
> to be dissed lands them in the cemetery: some grass,
> some flowers, a whole lot of respectful silence.
>
> And nobody to look at you.[224]

The relationship of overaggressive behavior to professional sports was discussed by Bob Glauber of *The Sporting
News* when he wrote:

> Welcome to the world of NFL cheap shots and fisti-
> cuffs, where players show callous disregard for one
> another, where the risk of serious injury keeps ris-
> ing and where the league's attempts at correcting
> the problem have failed to have a significant effect.

---

[224] Donna Britt, Washington Post Writers Group, *Lexington* (KY) *Herald-Leader*, Dec. 5, 1994.

. . . The NFL needs to rid itself of flagrant hits from other players who don't understand the distinction between aggressiveness and viciousness. . . .[225]

One must suppose that it is yet to be reached, but a shoe commercial must certainly push the limit of encouraging this antisocial attitude and rebelliousness. It shows Dennis Rodman asking Santa Claus for some new shoes and being reminded by Santa that he led the NBA in personal fouls and ejections, didn't follow the rules, skipped practices, and was suspended by his team. Rodman lifts Santa off the floor, smiles and says, "But I led the league in rebounds." So Santa tells an elf, "Okay, give him the shoes." In a newspaper column, Terry Pluto discusses the commercial and quotes the reaction of Cleveland Cavaliers General Manager Wayne Embry, who asked "What kind of message is that?" Pluto continued:

Then Embry paused for a moment.

"Actually, I know exactly what they are doing," he said. "They are targeting the market of young African-American males. They are deliberately showing a player who is currently suspended for refusing to listen to his coaches, and they are holding him up as some kind of hero. They think young people will like him being a rebel. . . .

Embry believes that there is a cultural war taking place, that the African-American community can't let itself be destroyed by violence, crime and de-

[225] Bob Glauber, "The Sporting News," *Lexington* (KY) *Herald-Leader*, Nov. 20, 1994.

spair. He believes in discipline, values and giving
kids real heroes to emulate.[226]

The counterculture of aggression, drugs, sex and violence is not an appropriate sanctuary for young men and
women, black or white. The remedy for their frustration is
in "the American way." It is in school, in study, and in prepa-
ration to take advantage of the opportunities available to
them in America to a degree far greater than anywhere else
in the world. Their places in society must be found one by
one, in the same way as yours must be found. It won't be
given to you; nor to them. It cannot be taken by violence. It
must be earned.

Another counterculture is that of the "gays," as homosexuals have come to call themselves. Many now compare
the claims for "equality" by gays to the demand for civil
rights by blacks. They are wrong. Blacks are not black by
choice or because of their behavior. Behavior is a matter of
choice; and homosexuals are identified as such only by their
homosexual behavior. It is only their behavior which ties
them together; and that behavior is precisely what sets them
apart from the rest of society. They speak of their homo-
sexuality as an innocent "alternative lifestyle" and charac-
terize as homophobic those who refuse to see it as acceptable. But, from whatever point of view, the distinguishing
characteristic of their identity is their choice of behavior. So
the issue, fairly stated, is not a civil rights issue at all. The
issue is whether the larger community should be compelled
to accept and treat as innocent and proper a chosen type of
behavior which has been condemned in virtually every nation and culture throughout history. To accept such aberrant sexual behavior on the argument that "there is no dif-

---

[226] Terry Pluto, Knight-Ridder News Service, *Lexington* (KY) *Herald-
Leader*, Dec. 5, 1994.

ference" or that "the temptation is overwhelming" would require society to likewise condone unmarried propagation and adultery as well, with a resulting destruction of the very foundation of the family and the social order. The common ground essential to culture, for community development of values and encouragement of acceptable behavior patterns, is being severely undermined in the name of "diversity." Even the need for a common language is denied. A culture which once was referred to proudly as the "melting pot" of immigrants into a community of Americans is endangered by hyphenation into ethnic or racial groups, such as African-Americans, Italian-Americans, Chinese-Americans, Euro-Americans, and so on. "On every side today ethnicity is the cause of the breaking of nations," wrote Pulitzer Prize winning historian Arthur Schlesinger, Jr.,[227] who went on to deplore the hyphenation of Americans and said:

> The genius of America lies in its capacity to forge a single nation from peoples of remarkably diverse racial, religious, and ethnic origins. It has done so because democratic principles provide both the philosophical bond of union and practical experience in civic participation. The American Creed envisages a nation composed of individuals making their own choices and accountable to themselves, not a nation based on inviolable ethnic communities. The Constitution turns on individual rights, not on group rights. . . .[228]

Schlesinger concludes that "the bonds of cohesion in our

---

[227] Arthur M. Schlesinger, Jr., *The Disuniting of America* (New York: W. W. Norton & Co., 1992), p. 10.

[228] Ibid., p. 134. See also Moynihan, *Pandaemonium* (Infra), p. xi.

society are sufficiently fragile, or so it seems to me, that it makes no sense to strain them by encouraging and exalting cultural and linguistic apartheid."[229]

On the great seal of the United States is the motto: "E Pluribus Unum." Once all schoolchildren knew that this is Latin for "One From Many." It bespeaks community. It is the antithesis of the fragmentation which is bound to result from a retreat of each hyphenated American into the culture of his ancestors in an ill-advised response to what the "politically correct" have been calling "Eurocentrism." But Schlesinger puts it well when he writes:

> Whatever the particular crimes of Europe, that continent is also the source — the *unique* source — of those liberating ideas of individual liberty, political democracy, the rule of law, human rights, and cultural freedom that constitute our most precious legacy and to which most of the world today aspires. These are *European* ideas, not Asian, nor African, nor Middle Eastern ideas, except by adoption.[230]

Were it not for the company of Schlesinger and another well-recognized liberal, Daniel Patrick Moynihan, I might think that my views are held only by those of us who refuse to be intimidated into accepting the "politically correct." Moynihan's book *Pandaemonium*[231] makes the startling point that "there are today just eight states on earth which both existed in 1914 and have not had their form of government changed by violence since then."[232] In the foreword of

---

[229] Ibid., p. 138.
[230] Ibid., p. 127.
[231] Daniel Patrick Moynihan, *Pandaemonium* (Oxford, Oxford University Press, 1993).
[232] Ibid., p. 10.

Moynihan's book, Adam Roberts of Balliol College, Oxford,
echoes Schlesinger, saying:

> Being based, however imperfectly, on individual
> rather than group rights and on the idea of the melt-
> ing pot, the U.S.A. is often inclined to underestimate
> the elemental force of ethnic issues elsewhere.[233]

Moynihan writes about ethnicity in international politics; but his analysis of the dangers in the perpetuation of
tribal allegiances is applicable to domestic politics as well.
Indeed, he mentions the recent riots in Los Angeles, quotes
an English journalist as having said that "the United States
is unwinding strand by strand, rather like the Soviet Union,
Yugoslavia or Northern Ireland," and himself sounds the
alarm as follows:

> The current small-arms fighting in American cit-
> ies is bound to escalate in terms both of weaponry
> and of aggression against whites; a role reversal,
> but the same drama.[234]

He concludes on a rather plaintive note that "for the
moment the more pressing matter is simply to contain the
risk, to restrain the tendency to hope for too much, either of
altruism or of common sense."[235]

We must hope that the American way is not lost because of a mistaken notion that "tolerance" requires America
to accept any counterculture in the name of "diversity." Tolerance does not require acceptance of antisocial behavior,
no matter what its guise. Meanness is no less meanness

---

[233] Ibid., p. xi.
[234] Ibid., p. 23.
[235] Ibid., p. 173.

because it is in the sports arena. Children and young people must be protected from bullies, black or white; and "acting bad" must not become the norm because of intimidation.

Chapter Eleven

Equality, Equal Rights and Community Responsibilities

*T*he Declaration of Independence says that all men are created equal; and, in some respects, that statement is true. In many ways, however, we are not equal. Some people are good looking and some of us are not. Some people are athletic and some of us are klutzes. Some are rich and some are poor. Some are born to aristocracy and some not. Some people are strong and some are weak. Some people are smart and some are slow. Some are healthy and some are handicapped. The blanket statement that all men are created equal doesn't fit the facts.

But we are all equal in the sight of God, and we should all be equal before the law. The Declaration of Independence means that the strong should not bully the weak. It means that the rich should not oppress the poor. It means that every American should have the opportunity to use his time and talents to achieve his own realistic goals. Each American should have the opportunity to do his best and, if that is good enough in a competitive world, to succeed.

Before America was founded, there was a caste system throughout the world such as still exists in India. Those who were born to the aristocracy were favored and those who were born commoners had no escape. In America those barriers were broken down and the accident of birth was no longer to be the measure of one's worth.

The equality envisioned by the founders of this country can be produced only through the Rule of Law which was planted and nurtured in the New World by those who fled the injustice and oppressive ways of the Old. The Rule of Law is designed to protect the weak from the strong. But the Rule of Law will not make the poor rich nor the homely good looking. At its very best it can offer only equality of opportunity, not equality of outcome.

In their book *Free to Choose*[236], the Friedmans include a chapter titled "Created Equal," in which they have this to say:

> Much of the moral fervor behind the drive for equality of outcome comes from the widespread belief that it is not fair that some children should have a great advantage over others simply because they happen to have wealthy parents. Of course it is not fair. However, unfairness can take many forms. It can take the form of the inheritance of property — bonds and stocks, houses, factories; it can also take the form of the inheritance of talent — musical ability, strength, mathematical genius. The inheritance of property can be interfered with more readily than the inheritance of talent. But from an ethical point of view, is there any difference between the two? Yet many people resent the inheritance of property but not the inheritance of talent.

---

[236] Milton and Rose Friedman, *Free to Choose* (Harcourt Brace Jovanovich, 1980).

. . . Life is not fair. It is tempting to believe that government can rectify what nature has spawned. But it is also important to recognize how much we benefit from the very unfairness we deplore.[237]

In further discussing inequalities, the Friedmans correctly point out that many inequalities are the consequences of choices people make, i.e., either profitable consequences of investment risks or, perhaps, losses resulting from careless decision-making. They make the point that, even if there is resultant inequality, it is the decision-maker himself who should profit or suffer by his choices. That is fair.

I'm past 65 and thinking about retirement. I believe I'll go back to school. This time I'm going on a basketball scholarship. That sounds like fun to me. Now, I know I'm old and slow and out of shape, but I'm equal. I don't know beans about basketball, but I'm equal. They may have somebody else who can help the team, but I've got rights. They may say I'm fat and flabby because I've overeaten, but its only a behavioral problem, and I can't help it. Besides, I've got rights. I think I'll go to UK. They're more equal than Eastern, Morehead or Louisville. I might even join the ladies' team. Their locker room probably smells better, and I've got rights.

One shouldn't trivialize equal rights, but sometimes overemphasis makes the point. The same God who made us equal in His sight made us different from each other. Common sense tells us that we are not equal in all things. To say that we are is to deny reality.

One of the ancient Greeks or Romans, I forget who, told his son that "before we can engage in the systematic discussion of anything, we must first define our terms." That means to intelligently discuss "equal rights," we must look to definitions for the words. Furthermore, understanding requires

---

[237] Ibid., pp. 136, 137.

that ideas be examined in their relationship to time and circumstances; that is, in a "context."

First, "equal" does not mean "same." Even the same things may not be equal. Apples may differ in size, weight and color, but still be apples. If equality were an absolute, then children could vote, we would all be skinny, and everybody's pay would be the same. That's nonsense.

On the other hand, if the rich or powerful always could have their way because of their greater resources, then our environment would be a jungle rather than a civilization. Regardless of inequality in wealth or power, a civilized society must provide for equality among its people, at least in the sense that all are treated fairly by their government and none may be made to suffer unfairly at the hands of another. The issue is fairness rather than equality, and fairness itself is quite subjective.

The other word is "rights." It is a word which has been stretched by repeated redefinition, and disconnected from what was once its necessary correlative, which is responsibility. In this country we revere that magnificent language: "We hold these truths to be self-evident; that all men are created equal; that they are endowed by their Creator with certain unalienable rights; that among these are life, liberty, and the pursuit of happiness." That language makes the words "equal" and "unalienable rights" sound as if they were absolutes. If they were, we would have no need for jails and no controversy over capital punishment, because no one could be deprived of his liberty or life. But that was the Declaration of Independence. Some years later, when it came to the Constitution, the people agreed that life, liberty and property might be taken from one by the state. Those accused of crime have only the right to "due process of law"; and even that may be waived.

So, we are not always equal and our rights are not absolute. This means that we must examine both "equal" and "rights" in the context of the time and circumstances in which those words are used.

Are all men equal before God in their relationship to Him? Yes. Women, too? Yes. Are all men equal before the bar of justice? Yes. From whatever ethnic background? Yes. Do all citizens have the same vote? Yes. Every faith? Yes.

The trouble comes when efforts are made in the name of "equal rights" to make unequals equal in the context of economics and social affairs.

First, let us look to the propriety of claiming "equal rights" in the world of commerce. As a practical matter, business will not work in a competitive marketplace unless the manager can hire capable and productive employees. If the manager cannot terminate incompetent and undependable employees, his business is likely to fail; and the jobs of all his employees go with it. Therefore, the successful manager must necessarily have the right to exercise judgment and discrimination in choosing and retaining his employees.

But, in the United States, it is well accepted that the manager should not discriminate against employees on the sole basis of their race, color, gender or creed. Discrimination on a basis wholly unrelated to business needs is unfair; and, in most cases, the law forbids it. This is not because everybody is "equal"; but because employees should not be treated unfairly.

In our present environment an issue is sometimes drawn between "affirmative action" and the creation or preservation of a "meritocracy." There is substantial political support for "affirmative action," which is premised in the history of unfair treatment of black people. Discrimination against people on the basis of their color in public affairs and employment is unlawful today. It now carries with it certain civil penalties, and sometimes even injunctive relief. Yet there are some who would go beyond those "civil rights" laws and try to deal with past wrongs through rem-

edies extracted today from people who themselves are innocent, or at the expense of other employees who are innocent. This is done by giving preferential treatment in employment and promotion to African-Americans. How can it
be fair to give preference today to someone not subjected to
unlawful discrimination, at the expense of his contemporary co-employee who was not guilty of unlawful discrimination? That also happens when black applicants to professional schools are given preference over better-qualified
applicants of other races. And what does that say about the
professions themselves when less qualified people are
trained instead of better qualified?

Except in a business directly related to the characteristic at issue, how can it make sense for a business enterprise to choose its employees or its leaders on the basis of:

• Good looks;
• Hair color;
• Sex;
• Ethnicity, or;
• Anything other than merit?

If preference is given to any individual as against another equally or better qualified individual, it seems only
right that the preference should be related to the needs of
the business. "Affirmative action" for blacks is as much discrimination as is giving preferences to those who are not black.

This is not to be taken as an endorsement of the Ku
Klux Klan or to foster hate for others of a different race,
religion or ethnic background. Let's be absolutely clear. Racism is an affront to God, who made all of us. The Bible says,
"he who oppresses the poor reproaches his Maker, but he
who is gracious to the needy honors Him."[238] How can this

[238] Proverbs 14: 31 (NAS); and see Proverbs 17: 5 to the same effect.

principle be different when applied to those of another color — any color? Regardless of the law, the measure of our duty is love for others — all others. The point here is that love for one person is not a proper reason to mistreat another.

A second area in which the expression "equal rights" is inappropriately used is that of private social organizations. There is understandable resentment when efforts are made in the name of "equal rights" to force intrusion of the uninvited into private social groups. Name-calling is the result. For example, men who seek to preserve the atmosphere of male-only social groups are the target of some females screaming the epithet "male chauvinist pigs" at them. This is hard to understand, because some of the same screamers also scream about their own "right to privacy."

The measure of "equal rights" is common sense and fairness in the context of their assertion.

Finally, and not of the least importance, is the separation of the concept known as "rights" from its correlative concept: "responsibilities." There are few, if any, rights without correlative responsibilities. The citizen who claims the right to vote has the responsibility to exercise that right in an honest and intelligent fashion. He should have no right to a vote which he sells, no matter what the price or how it is paid. Those who are uninformed should not be encouraged to vote. The citizen who claims the right to equal justice under law, should bear the responsibility of himself complying with the law. So, he has a responsibility to serve as a juror, and to provide evidence in court when he is a witness. A man who expects his country to defend him against its enemies has the responsibility to serve in the military forces when Uncle Sam points to him. An employee who claims the right to nondiscriminatory treatment by his employer has the responsibility to serve loyally and productively.

No society can promise "rights" without requiring responsible exercise of those rights.

Most grandfathers with whom I talk believe that the United States of America is the greatest nation ever seen on the face of this earth. But they also think that it was far greater when we grandfathers were in our teens and twenties. Younger people smile knowingly or snicker when their elders talk about "the good old days." They suspect that imagination has gilded the good, and that we have simply forgotten the bad times. They scoff at the idea that life without television and computer games could have been worthwhile. Science has its place, of course; but technology cannot replace the sense of community we have lost. Because we lived then and now, grandfathers may be in a better position than the generations which came after us to make a judgment about the relative happiness experienced then and now.

Most of today's grandfathers grew up during the "Great Depression." Many of our families were poor. You may think it strange, but my own parents never owned a house. During the Depression, my father was often unemployed. He tried to find work. Sometimes he had a part-time job. Sometimes he was "self-employed." When he finally got a job, he demonstrated his capabilities by holding middle-management positions and doing them well. During the Depression my mother worked, selling life insurance and furnishing most of the support for our family in that fashion. We were never "on relief," which is what welfare was then called. With the help of our extended family and with all of us pitching in to help, we children didn't even know we were poor. Times of adversity seem to be the times in which character is built; and shared suffering seems to strengthen community.

Then came World War II when the people of the United States responded to an attack on Pearl Harbor and the need to put down tyranny in Europe and the Pacific, even at the cost of thousands upon thousands of its young men. The survivors of that war are the grandfathers of today.

We think the difference between those days and these is a difference of spirit. In those days of depression and war, we enjoyed a spirit of community in the United States. That spirit of community has been all but lost in the demand for more and more individual or group "rights" and the turning away from community responsibilities.

Don't misunderstand me. There is no doubt but that citizens of this great country have rights which are unknown in many other countries; and those rights are precious to us all. Even so, in the name of "rights" we have seen develop a self-centered people who manifest decreasing concern for the welfare of others. Many people seem to have forgotten that one must give up some rights for the benefit of his community; that citizens have responsibilities as well as rights; and that the good of the community is a proper purpose for self-sacrifice. Indeed, if all its people were self-centered, the community could not survive. It would have no spirit to serve as its bond.

The very word "community" means people living together. A "community spirit" binds them together so that they can live peacefully, with each making a contribution for the benefit of all and each having a better life because of the contributions of the others. A community spirit requires a degree of selflessness on the part of the people; while the continual din created by louder and louder demands for "rights" manifests self-centeredness which is counter to community.

What would commerce be like without accepted standards of weights and measures? But apart from commerce, are there no measures of community values? No scales? No yardstick?

Are there no community standards? May television and movies and other media pander to any of the baser instincts of mankind? May they portray as acceptable — or even the norm — whatever behavior excites or titillates any audience, all in the name of "free" expression of "ideas?"

Is it to the best interests of either the individual or the community to permit behavior without limits or standards — in the name of "freedom"?

May those who are so inclined lie, steal, or cheat — in the name of "free enterprise"?

The community itself must share the burden of dealing with those who are not given appropriate community standards of behavior with which they are expected to comply. So it is that the destruction of standards of behavior has been followed by widespread increases in poverty, misery and crime.

When I speak of community standards of behavior, I do not mean "style," which itself is only superficial and changes with the seasons. On the contrary, I speak of a community's expectations concerning the appropriate behavior of people in the community.

A community is composed of the people who live in the same locality or place and necessarily share time, space and infrastructure with each other. They have common interests, including those common interests related to peace, order and safety. Depending on the circumstances and context, a "community" may be a neighborhood, a city, or even a whole country. The people may have grown up together; or they may have moved together from one place to another, as did the pioneers who settled the United States; or they may have come from different places with different cultural backgrounds. But now they live together in an identifiable community. Those in a community have many interests in common. Together they need to provide the structure which will accommodate their living in proximity with one another. A part of that structure is physical, such as roads and bridges and utilities. A second part is a system by which some common needs such as police and fire protection or garbage and sewage disposal may be met. Not the least important of the community structure is a general understanding and consensus of the kinds of actions and behavior which will be tolerated by the community. These become the standards by which behavior is either condoned or condemned.

As we have seen, some of the community standards, usually those which are minimal in their requirements, are enacted into law and form the predicate for punishment if they be not obeyed.

Although it is frequently said that we cannot make people be nice to each other, that blanket statement is not wholly true. Everybody is insecure; and everybody wants to be respected, and even loved. Those basic psychological truths are the foundation for a community's enforcement of its standards, quite apart from punishment by fine or imprisonment. Community standards can be enforced by the psychological effect of community approval or disapproval. Except for those who are pretentiously rebellious and attach themselves to a subgroup in the community for purposes of psychic security, most people will comply with community standards so that they do not feel community disapproval.

Community standards become such after the people have seen the consequences of certain behavior and thereupon developed a consensus as to whether that behavior is helpful or harmful to the people or to the community itself. When people can see the benefit of some particular behavior, they will encourage its replication in many ways, including at the least simply praise and commendation. On the other hand, behavior which is seen to be harmful to a miscreant's family, friends, or others can be discouraged by disapproval, whether spoken or simply sensed.

Chapter Twelve

Learning, Common Sense and Wisdom

*A*ll of us start life completely ignorant. The baby knows nothing. He must rely on only his instincts and the kindness of others for food, shelter and clothing. But we learn, and we gain the knowledge that permits us to care for ourselves. Even animals do this. Everybody who lives, learns. What we learn may be good or bad, helpful or harmful, worthwhile or not; but we all learn. Learning is sometimes thought of as "education"; but to think of learning only in relation to classrooms and schools is to understand only a small part of the whole experience.

We learn by acquiring information, processing it, and storing it in our memories. Probably the easiest element is acquisition in that we are virtually inundated with information throughout our waking hours. Our own senses (sight, hearing, touch, smell and taste) provide information from our surroundings which enable us to learn from our own experience. We also learn from the experience of others, including family, friends and even strangers. We acquire information by way of books, media and many other channels of communication. This offers us learning from the experience of others.

While one may well disagree with their conclusions, the Tofflers[239] pique our interest with their "Third Wave" theory. They tell us that the agricultural revolution gave way to the industrial revolution which itself is now giving way to the "Third Wave" or "today's gigantic upheaval in the knowledge base of society."[240] They say:

> While land, labor, raw materials and capital were the main factors of production in the Second Wave economy of the past, knowledge — broadly defined here to include data, information, images, symbols, culture, ideology and values — is now the central resource of the Third Wave economy.[241]

Learning is more than knowledge of raw facts. Learning implies understanding, which is "to perceive and comprehend the nature and significance" of the facts.[242] Facts can be absorbed by rote. But if the facts are not understood there is no true learning, because there is no way by which the facts may be utilized. Understanding or comprehension requires evaluation.

Back, then, to Professor Drucker who deals with his own question: "What is knowledge?" He writes:

> Academia defines knowledge as what gets printed. But surely this is not knowledge; it is raw data. Knowledge is information that changes something

[239] Alvin and Heidi Toffler, *Creating a New Civilization* (Atlanta: Turner Publishing, Inc., 1994).
[240] Ibid., p. 36.
[241] Ibid., p. 42.
[242] *The American Heritage Dictionary.*

or somebody — either by becoming grounds for action, or by making an individual (or an institution) capable of different and more effective action.[243]

Again, he says: "Information is data endowed with relevance and purpose. Converting data into information thus requires knowledge."[244]

Far more difficult than information acquisition is the evaluation of the information. First, we must be selective in giving our attention to only that information which is of greatest significance. Sometimes this is very difficult because of the distractions which bombard our senses. Sometimes it is choosing which of several books to read or even choosing to read instead of watching television. The second task is to analyze the information and determine whether it is worthy of attention. Obviously this analysis requires some criteria as to worth. For example, much of the information thrust upon us by the television industry is trash, wholly worthless, not even worthwhile as entertainment. Then thirdly, one must evaluate the information in terms of its relationship to context and in terms of its relationship to other knowledge already remembered. This is essential to comprehension or understanding. Another example: because we think in images, television produces the illusion of truth, and it must be related to its context and other knowledge to make a determination as to its truth and accuracy.

Finally, learning requires that one store in his memory that information which has significance and has been understood. Indeed, if the information is "memorable" it may be necessary to give it special study or to memorize it so as to minimize the chances that it will be later forgotten. Again, standards of relative value or priorities must be used to make

[243] Drucker, *New Realities*, p. 251.
[244] Ibid., p. 209.

these decisions. Otherwise, the mind and memory is cluttered with meaningless trivia and is not so well able to process other information later acquired.

Again and again you will hear confusing messages from people who use language loosely, even learned people. Understand that words have different meanings and should be carefully chosen and used. The adjective "learned" may mean much the same as "educated," but neither means "smart." "Smart" is like "intelligent" but not the same as "wise." Some people are smarter than others. They more quickly grasp the meaning of abstractions, and apply them to reality. This is true both inside and outside the classroom. Some people with little classroom education have remarkable common sense. Common sense is the natural ability to apply what one has learned to real life situations, wherever and by whatever means the learning was acquired.

Many learned people have great difficulty coping with the real world. They do foolish things. They are scoffed at and sometimes referred to as "educated fools." They have little common sense. On the other hand, there are those with native intelligence and little education who seem able to make good judgments and to cope well with everyday living. They do this through inborn common sense, even if they have little "book learning." Most of them do well in life and some are eminently successful in the business world.

That part of our learning which we acquire in the schoolroom can be called "formal education." It is not to be taken lightly. Learning to read and to write enables us to communicate with others, and this enables us to exchange thoughts and ideas. The better we develop our communication skills, the better we can interact with other people in family, social, business, and other affairs. Communication may be the most important of all the skills we can develop.

Quite as important as the words we use is the cultural context in which they are used. Without that cultural context there is likely to be lack of understanding or even mis-understanding. This is what E. D. Hirsch, Jr., wrote about in his book, titled *Cultural Literacy*. It is the "grasp of background information that writers and speakers assume their readers already have," to quote from the dust jacket of his book.[245] So schools should teach and you should study geography, history, literature, philosophy and art. These subjects give us the background for the intelligent communication of ideas. Before television, people read books. Even with television, discerning people read books. Biography, history, "how-to-do-it," personal growth, technical subjects, business and investments, et cetera, et cetera, et cetera; all can be found in books. Fiction for children and adults, an opening of the vistas of imagination, is the promise of books. Before Gutenberg, only a few people were literate and books were scarce. His invention of movable type for the printing press changed the world as hardly any other invention, before or since.

You should develop a love affair with books. But, be selective. Don't waste your time on trash. I've read somewhere that television is stealing our children's lives, one half hour at a time. Books can steal time, too, if they are not selected with care. Choose the classics, which are time-proven. Read those books which have had their value — in both subject matter and style — endorsed by generations of readers. Insofar as contemporary books are concerned, read those by well-respected authors and those which are recommended by well-respected critics.

Read carefully. If at first you don't understand a passage, reread it until you do. If after real effort you still can't understand, you may be "in over your head" and should try something more elementary until you are ready for the book at hand. Maybe not. If the author is too obtuse to communi-

[245] E. D. Hirsch, Jr., *Cultural Literacy: What Every American Needs to Know* (Boston: Houghton Mifflin Co., 1987).

cate with his readers, get a book by a better author. Authors are not blessed equally with the talent of communication; and some are better than others.

Read critically. That doesn't mean to read negatively; it means to think while you read. What are the author's sources? He has no right to get his facts wrong. Are his premises valid? Are his conclusions sound? Remember, the book sets out only the author's opinions; and the fact that they are in print does not mean that all his opinions are correct. It is all right to be a skeptic; but don't be a cynic. A skeptic questions what he hears and reads, in an effort to find the truth. A cynic distrusts everything he hears or reads; and everybody. He believes that none but himself is motivated by virtue. His cynicism doesn't lead to truth so much as it leads to misery.

Many books, like this one, use footnotes or "endnotes" or other references to "authorities," which range from the Bible, to Shakespeare, to current authors and so on. These citations to "authorities" have two purposes. First, they may add credibility to the book being read. Second, they offer the reader a reference to another relevant source, so that he may pursue the issue further. There are at least two views as to value of such citations. Zacharias writes:

> How can one possibly prescribe a moral principle, or the lack of one, without justifying the authority of the source? And yet, this is the level at which so many issues are argued.[246]

But this invites the extension of the argument into further argument, this time on the relative authority of sources, including a comparison of their other writings. On the other hand, Thomas a' Kempis wrote:

---

[246] Zacharias, *Can Man Live Without God?*, p. 14.

Let not the authority of the writer be a stumbling block, whether he be of great or small learning; but let the love of pure truth draw thee to read. Inquire not who spoke this or that, but mark what is spoken.[247]

He brings us back to the principle that we must think while we read. In doing so, we may very well attribute greater weight to the thoughts of one author than to those of another. To do so we must weigh each in the balance against credibility and judgment.

Use books. Internalize the worthwhile things you learn, and let them serve you. If you have a challenge, a task about which you are uncertain, find a book. "How-to-do-it" books are available for every task from raising a garden to managing a business. Find a book or two which relate to your challenge, and you will have help, perhaps even expert help. Get a library card, and use it.

But learning itself is not the ultimate goal. Of even greater importance is wisdom. It is wisdom which leads one to make the right choices, which produce good consequences for oneself, his family and his community. Wisdom is an "understanding of what is true, right or lasting."[248] It is "common sense, good judgment."[249]

The Proverbs speak extensively of knowledge, understanding and wisdom, saying:

The beginning of wisdom is: acquire wisdom;[250]

How much better it is to get wisdom than gold! And to get understanding is to be chosen above silver. [251]

---

[247] Thomas a' Kempis, *Of the Imitation of Christ*, Book I, Chapter V, p. 17. (New York: Thomas Nelson & Sons, 1931).
[248] *The American Heritage Dictionary.*
[249] Ibid.
[250] Prov. 4: 7. (NAS)
[251] Prov. 16: 16. (NAS)

The fear of the Lord is the beginning of wisdom, . . .[252]

For the Lord gives wisdom; from His mouth come knowledge and understanding.[253]

You can be wise. In fact, God promises wisdom to those who ask for it.[254] Wisdom is made up of learning, common sense, and the ability to discern what is right or wrong. Wisdom has a proper system of values.

Moral education" today has fallen into disrepute. . . . To slough off moral values as modern education proposes to do only means that education conveys the wrong values. It conveys indifference, irresponsibility, cynicism. Precisely what the moral values of education in the knowledge society have to be will be hotly debated. But education in moral values, and the commitment to moral values, will be central. Knowledge people have to learn to take responsibility.[255]

Wisdom is given a voice in the eighth chapter of Proverbs, where "she" says:

For my mouth will utter truth; and wickedness is an abomination to my lips.[256]

I, wisdom, dwell with prudence, and I find knowledge and discretion.[257]

---

[252] Prov. 9: 10. (NAS)
[253] Prov. 2: 6. (NAS)
[254] James 1: 5.
[255] Drucker, *New Realities*, p. 238.
[256] Prov. 8: 7. (NAS)
[257] Prov. 8: 12. (NAS)

Counsel is mine and sound wisdom; I am understanding, power is mine.[258]

I walk in the way of righteousness, in the midst of the paths of justice . . .[259]

Wisdom is consistent with truth, and it relates judgment to morals and ethics. It is good to be learned. It is better to be learned and understanding. It is best to be learned, understanding and wise.

While each generation needs to see and understand wisdom in the circumstances of its own time, wisdom is not new to this generation. Instead, whatever wisdom is expressed today — whether spoken or written — is an echo from the past, in the circumstances of the present. Of course, that is why study of the liberal arts is meaningful; and that is why we still learn wise lessons from the Bible, even though it was written centuries ago. In all that time, human nature hasn't changed.

Sadly, in recent years teachers in our country's public schools have been encouraged — sometimes even required — to serve up "value-neutral" education to their students. Many of them refuse to teach the difference between right and wrong, for fear that someone will complain in the name of "cultural diversity" and even sue. Some even teach "do what feels good" and "don't criticize," so everybody will have "self-esteem."

For years I have bemoaned the fact that in the public schools children were not taught how to make decisions. Now with "reform" in the public schools, they are teaching "decision-making."[260] But the cure may be worse than the dis-

---

258 Prov. 8: 14. (NAS)
259 Prov. 8: 20. (NAS)
260 William Kilpatrick, *Why Johnny Can't Tell Right from Wrong* (New York: Simon and Schuster, 1993).

ease. As decision-making is now taught, it is "value free" decision-making, so that everybody will be non-judgmental. What good does it do to teach a youngster the best way to make decisions if he will use that newly-learned skill to rob a liquor store, the morality of which his non-judgmental teacher has left him to judge for himself?

It is essential that you learn to think for yourself, and you must learn to make your own choices. Your thought processes and choices should be value driven — they should include consideration of moral and ethical values. Schoolteachers should help children learn these values; and children should not be confused with hypothetical questions that suggest answers which violate the moral and ethical standards their parents have taught them.

Of course, I know that those who advocate "value neutral" education say that values should be taught by the family. That is not really the point. *All* of us believe that parents should teach moral and ethical values to their children. The point is that those moral and ethical values should be reinforced by the schools and the community. The family is not the only place where goodness, truth and virtue should be taught. What father or mother can justify objections to teaching their child goodness, truth and virtue? A stable and civil community can be built and maintained only if its families, schools and the community itself all work together to instill the proper moral, ethical and spiritual values in its children.

Moreover, some young people come from families which have no values. If they are not taught ethics and morality in their families, where will they learn? Surely the schools would be better than the street or the jailhouse. Surely the community, which is itself at risk, may properly insist that its youngsters be taught the moral values upon which the community depends.

Much of what I perceive to be wrong in the elementary and secondary public schools is a product of institutions of higher learning, thc colleges of education which teach young people to be teachers. I certainly do not condemn all teachers at any level, nor do I call for the abolition of universities and teachers' colleges. My concern is to identify some of the excesses of academe and to urge that corrective measures be instituted. Hopefully, there is time to restore the luster higher education once had; and deserved.

As related by Reginald G. Damerell[261], in 1984 the Harvard Graduate School of Education held an international conference to deal with "new and disturbing evidence" of deterioration in teenagers' "inferential comprehension." Damerell, himself a professor for more than a decade, continued:

> This latest evidence of decline had touched off a new movement among educationists — to teach thinking skills as a discrete subject.
>
> The establishment of this new barony aptly illustrates how educationists turn an old failure into a new success. Having diminished ability to read with reading skills, they introduced remedial reading. Having undermined ability to compute with math skills, they introduced remedial math. Having diminished the ability to write, they introduced writing skills. For students no longer able to follow verbal instructions, they introduced listening skills. Having diminished all that contributes to thinking, educationists would now try to teach thinking skills.[262]

Academe is a self-created structure, ostensibly designed

---

[261] Reginald G. Damerell, *Education's Smoking Gun* (New York: Freundlich Books, 1985).
[262] Ibid., 251.

to benefit students. Instead it has developed so as to benefit professors and, not coincidentally, the administrative wing of the education establishment. It is full of experts, with their own jargon. But jargon is not wisdom and experts can be dangerous, because they can lead the non-expert into error through jargon, half-truth, or outright deception.

Another former college teacher, Newt Gingrich, recently wrote:

> . . . Put simply, higher education in this country is out of control. First, campuses are run for the benefit of the faculty, not the students. Second, tenured faculty have become increasingly out of touch with the rest of America, rejecting the culture of the people who pay their salaries. Third, there is an acceptance of higher costs without effective management by administrators.[263]

Some of the attitudes of academe today are the inheritance of the sixties, when most of the institutions of higher education were taken over by the students in a rebellion against authority — government, institutional, societal and moral. The students were abetted by young faculty, and standards were dissolved. Allan Bloom, who was a professor at Cornell during that period, has this to say:

> About the sixties it is now fashionable to say that although there were indeed excesses, many good things resulted. But, so far as universities are concerned, I know of nothing positive coming from that period; it was an unmitigated disaster for them . . .[264]

---

[263] Newt Gingrich, *To Renew America* (New York: HarperCollins, 1995), p. 219.
[264] Bloom, *Closing of the American Mind*, p. 320.

He goes on:

> The reforms were without content, made for the
> "inner-directed" person. They were an acquiescence
> in a leveling off of the peaks, and were the source
> of the collapse of the entire American educational
> structure, recognized by all parties when they talk
> about the need to go "back to the basics." This col-
> lapse is directly traceable to both the teachings and
> the deeds of the universities in the sixties . . .[265]

Gingrich puts it this way:

> Most tenured positions in higher education are how
> held by passionate advocates of the anti-Vietnam war
> movement. These former radicals have now become
> the comfortable, all-purpose "deconstructionists" of
> American culture.[266]

After relating some specific examples of recent university faculty attitudes and actions, he writes:

> Given this academic bias, is it any wonder Ameri-
> can civilization and its values are not being trans-
> mitted to the next generation?[267]

Much of the present condition is the result of persistent
cries from the faculty for "academic freedom." They do not
mean just free speech, in the sense that every citizen shares
that constitutional right. They mean instead that college
professors must be permitted to teach whatever they see

---

[265] Ibid., p. 321.
[266] Gingrich, *To Renew America*, p. 220.
[267] Ibid.

fit. So, even though the taxpayers furnish a major part of the financial support of the public universities, they claim that we have no right to expect from the professors that they teach our children truth and honor, or even that they teach the values upon which civil order is founded.

Research was once justified because professors were teachers first and properly kept abreast of the fields in which they taught. That has changed. Tenure and job security, — and promotion through the academic ranks — is now directly related to the number of papers one has had published. Publication implies that one has discovered something never before known. Now the academics' need to publish leads to "research" or "science" which sometimes borders on the ridiculous. Hence the "explosion of knowledge" is an accumulation of minutiae, much of which is of little value to other than the professor and the publisher. Professors should be judged not upon whether they have "discovered" something, but whether they have discovered something worthwhile. They should be judged not upon whether they have "added to the body of knowledge"; but whether they have made a valuable addition to knowledge.

Nowadays, "hard" science finds that a massive overdose of, say, peanut butter causes cancer in rats; one of scores of journals, anxious to fill its pages and justify its existence, accepts for publication a "learned" paper describing the rats' reaction to an overdose of peanut butter; and the public media — ever on the lookout for "news" — treats the paranoid public to another cancer scare. This is not because peanut butter causes cancer in people, but because some researcher had a special interest in peanut butter and rats, — or perhaps because he could find no other published paper on that subject.

The drive to "publish or perish" in order to obtain tenure or academic promotions is apparently what leads university faculty members to write beyond the farthest stretch of their imaginations and thereby avoid duplication of research papers already published by others. Unwarranted conclusions are drawn from inadequate information or inappropriate investigations. Every day some scientist discovers that something which another scientist thought was true is not. One mistake of theoreticians is in trying to fit human nature into their abstractions rather than in fitting their theories to human nature.

Today's universities trace their heritage back to the development of the "scientific method" and to the "age of enlightenment." The scientific method is defined as:

> The totality of principles and processes regarded as characteristic of or necessary for scientific investigation, including rules for concept formation, conduct of observations and experiments, and validation of hypotheses by observations or experiments.[268]

In more elementary terms, the scientific method is used to test a scientist's theory by observation or experiments. This method of inquiry is well adapted to the natural sciences and has led to the marvelous development of science and technology evident today. So far, so good. My complaint is that the scientific method has been utilized in today's universities more to support scientists than to support valid scientific inquiry.

The salaries of tenured professors who spend little time in the classroom, their "perks," and the need to support armies of graduate students performing research and teaching undergraduate classes have led to the need for extraordinarily large funding of today's universities. This funding is sought from various sources because tuition alone will

---

[268] *The American Heritage Dictionary.*

not support the faculty and administration of any institution of higher learning. Much of the support comes from
government, with direct subsidies at both the state and local levels. Large parts of the funding is through research
expenditures of the federal government. In constant dollars,
federal obligations to universities and colleges grew from
$11.8 billion in 1980 to $13.6 billion in 1990; then to $15.9
billion in 1992.[269] That is an increase of 15% in ten years
and another 17% in the next two years. During roughly the
same period, total research expenditures of all colleges and
universities rose from $8.8 billion in 1981 to $14.5 billion in
1990 (65%) and to $16.8 billion in 1994, another 16%.[270] All
of this is after adjustments for inflation, so the increases
are real.

Many scientists never get out of school. They get baccalaureate degrees, obtain employment as graduate students
doing research for their professors, obtain their own graduate degrees, and themselves become the next generation of
professors. Many of them never experience the real world.
But they and their colleagues need students, undergraduate and graduate students, in order to justify the very existence of their academic institution, — not to say to pay
their salaries. If there are too few American students who
make the grade, they recruit overseas.

Of the doctoral degrees conferred by universities in the
United States, the percentage granted to foreign citizens
grew from 16.4% in 1980 to 31.6% in 1993. This is to say
that almost one-third of the doctorates conferred in 1993 by
our universities went to foreign graduate students.[271] Even
more amazing, 59.4% of engineering doctorates went to foreign citizens; as did 55.2% of those in mathematics, and

---

[269] U. S. Census Bureau, *Statistical Abstract: 1996*, Table No. 964.
[270] Ibid., Table No. 963.
[271] U. S. Census Bureau, *Statistical Abstact: 1995*, Table No. 997.

50.5% of those in the computer sciences. On the other end of the spectrum, U. S. citizens were granted 62.6% of the doctorates in the "earth sciences," 69% in the biological sciences (which include botany and zoology), 59.9% in the social sciences, and 92.8% in psychology.[272]

Academic scientists study by defining and redefining classifications after observing differences and similarities so as to create different categories. This is done to set the stage for statistical analysis, the researchers' tool *par excellence*. They identify variables, postulate relationships, apply statistics, and write another paper to be submitted for publication.

One must remember that science is not man's creation of nature's laws and forces, but only their discovery. Then, sometimes, inventors develop a way to make use of such natural laws and forces. Indeed, sometimes inventors can make use of nature's laws and forces without discovery of anything more than their effect. Science is truly discovery, — that some scientific hypotheses are consistent with nature and some not.

"Scientism" is the theory that investigational methods used in the natural sciences should be applied in all fields of inquiry. Those who promote scientism include behavioral scientists who presume to explain in learned papers the whys of normal as well as abnormal behavior. When their theories are thin, they simply redefine normality and write more papers. Reading the papers and books of behavioral scientists carries a temptation to try to find oneself in or among their classifications, and then to see how their research is applied to oneself. The risk involved is in shackling oneself to the researcher's classifications and conclusions. This leads to confining your future to his theories. Read critically, as I have said elsewhere. If you see in the writings of social sci-

---

[272] Ibid.

entists descriptions of tendencies which you recognize in
yourself, let that recognition free you from the unacceptable; but do not let it serve to identify you as a victim and
thereby limit your choices in life.

In many ways we are at the mercy of academe. We learn
many things at a teacher's knee. If they teach us untruths,
we are misled but likely to accept in innocence what we are
taught. For one example, professional educators are now
selling "inventive spelling" by which young children are permitted to spell words in whatever way the children think
the words are spelled. The ostensible purpose is to teach
these children to write; but, if they spell any way they like,
they will not be able to read or to look up an unfamiliar
word in the dictionary.

So we see that those who serve in "institutions of higher
learning" are not necessarily wise, and should be judged one
by one. So-called "higher learning" does not equate with
wisdom; and neither academics nor scientists are necessarily wise.

Wisdom requires values. Without values there may be
intelligence, reason, genius and even intellectuality; but not
wisdom. Wisdom depends on values for its prudence, sagac-
ity and virtue. Wisdom produces values-driven choices. So
it is that James wrote:

> But the wisdom from above is first pure, then peace-
> able, gentle, reasonable, full of mercy and good
> fruits, unwavering, without hypocrisy.[273]

---

[273] James 3: 17. (NAS)

Chapter Thirteen

Measuring Yourself

*H*ow should you measure yourself? How may you as-
sess your worth as a person? By good looks, athletic
ability, intellect or wealth? By comparison with somebody
else; and, if so, whom? By your popularity? Before you answer "yes" to any of the above, read on.

Mental images are an essential part of our thought processes. Words create images in our minds; so our attitudes,
beliefs and behavior are directly related to our mental images and the words which produce them. One must be very
careful to make clear distinctions between words so that his
thinking is not muddled with overlapping mental images.

An expression often used nowadays is "self-esteem." It
sounds almost like "self-respect" and "self-confidence"; and
many people can't make the distinctions among them. There
are, however, profound differences.

In the now-popular sense of that term, "self-esteem"
has come to excuse the failure to discipline children and to
justify unwarranted praise. If children are not required to

work, they will play. I suspect that most of them are smarter than the child psychologists who would require no effort from them for fear that they might be embarrassed if somebody else does better. Self-esteem simply means feeling good about oneself. There may be good reason for self-esteem; or there may not be. For parents or teachers to praise a child and try to increase his self-esteem when he has done nothing deserving of praise is counterproductive to that child's future welfare. Such a child is misled into believing that he is entitled to praise regardless of accomplishment, or even without effort on his part to successfully accomplish what is expected of him. As a result he is baffled, perplexed and even resentful when he fails because of his own lack of effort. This euphemism, "self-esteem," is also a predicate for value-neutral education, about which I have had more to say elsewhere. It leads to a lack of self-discipline and to the expectation of reward without merit. It is the psychological underpinning of the current "victim" mentality, by which nobody takes responsibility and everybody pleads victimization. It is pernicious in its influence on children who should be encouraged to earn self-respect by integrity and achievement, instead of being congratulated for their lack of effort. I hope you understand the difference between self-respect and "self-esteem"; because, if you earn the former, nobody can take it from you, and the latter is wholly dependent on the praise of others. Self-respect fosters independence, while "self-esteem" is really dependent on other people.

All of us would like to be respected. Respect is in the manner by which others act toward you. If others are courteous, listening to and accepting your opinions, they manifest respect. They show by their attitude toward you whether you are held in favorable regard.

You are probably familiar with a comedian who has long earned his livelihood with the posture and protestation that

"I don't get no respect." You may know people who maintain a constant attitude of belligerence in the belief that belligerence begets respect. You may have seen young men who strut around with pistols, demanding respect. Some people whine for respect. Others just hang around wishing for it. None of these methods work. People may seem deferential to a belligerent person, or to a young man with a gun; but the deference is out of fear, rather than respect. Fear lasts only so long as there is an immediate threat. Respect endures.

Before others will respect you, you must first have self-respect. Self-respect is earned. It is earned by integrity and achievement. When we talk about the "integrity" of a thing, we mean the measure of whether it is whole, or sound, or complete. When we apply the term to a person, the idea is much the same; but it compares the person to values and standards of conduct. We think of his dependability, even in trying circumstances. We think of his credibility, even at the times when telling a falsehood would be profitable to him. We think of how he can be trusted to do what is right, even in secret.

Better is the poor who walks in his integrity, than
he who is crooked though he be rich.[274]

If you would respect yourself, you must first know in your own heart that you have integrity of character; which means that you adhere to high standards of conduct and behavior, and that you treat others as you would like to be treated by them.

We have examined the sources of moral and social values. We have identified virtues.[275] The question remaining

[274] Prov. 28: 6. (NAS)
[275] Virtue is defined as "moral excellence and righteousness; goodness." *The American Heritage Dictionary.*

is how you can make these values and virtues a part of your own life. As Aristotle said, "it is not enough to know what virtue is; we must strive to have and use it, and try whatever ways we may to become good."[276] This is done by internalizing and utilizing these moral values. Now don't think to yourself, "This is too hard. I'll do it someday, but not now." Don't walk away from the challenge. Remember, it is *your own* future life which is at stake; and *nobody else* can internalize and practice virtue for you. *You must do this for yourself.*

Is it worthwhile? All three of the western religions teach virtue as being related to God.[277] But the requirements of virtue are not so much for God's benefit as for the benefit of men and women who will obey the laws of God in a loving spirit. As we have seen, Aristotle concludes that virtue is essential to happiness.[278] It must be plain that a community depends upon its virtuous citizens for peace and the orderly conduct of its affairs, both public and private. What is more important than virtue? It cannot be vice, which is the antithesis of virtue. What rational person would rather be a slave to vice than enjoy freedom, the product of virtue?

Step one: go to the sources of moral values. Learn law from the Torah; learn love and forgiveness from the teachings of Jesus; learn about alms-giving from Islam. Read what the world's great philosophers have taught about ethics. Read the biographies of great and good men, whose lives are an example for us. Study virtue in these good sources. Listen to your parents, ministers, and teachers as they tell you how to be good. If you question what they teach you,

---

[276] Aristotle, (Classics Club ed.) *Nichomachean Ethics*, Book X, Chapter 10, p. 238.

[277] See *New Testament*: Phil. 4: 8; 2 Pet. 1: 3-11. See *Torah*: Exod. 15: 26; Deut. 26: 16-19. See *Quràn*: IV: 36-42; VII: 42-43; XVI: 97.

[278] Aristotle, (Classics Club ed.) *Nichomachean Ethics*, Book I, Chapters 10-11, pp. 94-98).

ask if it is consistent with the values you have learned from the written sources.

Step two: as you learn about moral values, internalize them. Make them a part of yourself. Develop the kind of conscience about which Isaiah spoke when he said:

> And your ears will hear a word behind you, "this is the way, walk in it," whenever you turn to the right or to the left.[279]

One learns in grammar school that to pass a "multiple choice" test, one must choose the correct answer from among the multiple choices available. In real life, the same principle applies, and the essential element in making the right choice is the application of the right moral values. In real life, choices are not always between what is right and what is wrong. Sometimes choices must be made between what is good and what is better, or what is bad and what is worse. If, however, you have internalized and practiced virtue, you can respond appropriately to this injunction:

> This above all: to thine own self be true, and it must follow, as the night the day, thou canst not then be false to any man.[280]

For the third step, let's turn again to Aristotle, who tells us of the need to practice virtue in order to develop the capacity and habit. He puts it in these words:

> It may fairly be said then that a just man becomes just by doing what is just, and a temperate man becomes temperate by doing what is temperate,

---

[279] Isa. 30: 21. (NAS)
[280] Shakespeare, *Hamlet*, Act I, Scene 3, Line 75.

and if a man did not so act, he would not have much
chance of becoming good. But most people, instead
of acting, take refuge in theorizing; they imagine
that they are philosophers and that philosophy will
make them virtuous; in fact, they behave like
people who listen attentively to their doctors but
never do anything that their doctors tell them. But
a healthy state of the soul will no more be produced
by this kind of philosophizing than a healthy state
of the body by this kind of medical treatment.[281]

He says that moral virtue is the outcome of habit[282] and
"a person's character is the result of the way in which he
exercises his capacities."[283]

One should *always* remember *never* to say "always" or
"never." Yet if that paradigm has an exception, it is that
one's integrity is always of the greatest importance to his
life. It is more important than riches, relationships, or even
reputation. It is what one sees in himself when he looks in
the mirror every morning. No matter what others may think
of him, he himself knows whether he has integrity. If one
knows that his actions are consistent with high standards
of conduct, he can hold his head high even in the face of
criticism by others. If he has lost his integrity, he feels secret shame even if others sing his praises.

Adopt for yourself and your behavior the highest moral
and ethical standards. Then live by them. Don't think that
there is some distance between integrity and corruption, or
that they form two ends of a continuum with plenty of room
between them for "a little bit of sin." Not so. If one surren-

---

[281] Aristotle, (Classics Club ed.) *Nichomachean Ethics*, Book II, Chapter 3, pp. 104-105.
[282] Ibid., Book II, Chapter 1, p. 100.
[283] Ibid., Book III, Chapter 7, p. 123.

ders to corruption, even a little bit, his integrity is impaired. The limits of integrity are fixed, not flexible. Theft of only one dollar breaches those limits as much as the theft of ten, or a thousand. As the Scriptures make it clear in the words of Jesus: "He who is faithful in a very little is faithful also in much; and he who is dishonest in a very little is dishonest also in much."[284]

In the courtroom we swear witnesses to tell "the truth, the whole truth, and nothing but the truth." This is because over the years we have learned that one can lie while telling a half-truth as well as by telling an untruth. Even concealment, or silence when there is a duty to speak are the same as lies. Tell the truth. Tell the truth all the time. If you tell the truth, you won't have to remember anything but the truth. Your credibility is very important to you. Your relationships with other people depend in great measure upon your credibility; and if it is ever impaired, it is extremely difficult to restore. Integrity requires truth; and anything more or less is a breach of the limits of integrity.

Practice honesty. Do not cheat. Even if cheaters win, they cannot be proud of having won by cheating; and they sacrifice their credibility and the respect of others. There are good things in sports; and bad things. Learning teamwork, sharing responsibilities, playing by the rules, and gaining the satisfaction of honest achievement are all good and worthwhile. But to overemphasize sports as if they were sufficiently important to win by any means is to risk distortion of the very character which competitive sports are meant to build. Do not believe the sports announcers, coaches and players who tell you that it's all right to cheat, "just don't get caught." They will desert you in a minute if you're caught; and you'll really be left alone, without them and without honorable people who despise cheating. Don't believe those

---

[284] Luke 16: 10. (RSV)

who would justify cheating by saying "everybody does it." They're wrong. Not everybody cheats. Cheating is destructive of character, and it leads to greater vices. Practice honesty.

Be honest. Do not take anything that belongs to somebody else. No matter how you try to excuse it, it is stealing. If people do not have a right to own property, what good to them are other rights?

Do what is right. Some people seem to think that "if it's legal, do it" but not everything legal is moral and ethical. To do right means to act in a moral and ethical manner, even if not required by law to do so.

Sometimes when you are making choices, one of the alternatives is inconsistent with your values — and you know it. It will have bad consequences, for you yourself or for somebody else; or it has a risk of harm; or it is just plain wrong. But it looks like fun; and other people do it; and your friends tease you to do it. Then you try to find a way to justify it, — to make an excuse to make the wrong choice. That is temptation at work; and it can be hard to turn to the right choice.

Temptations can relate to any of your values and can present themselves in many different forms. You may be tempted to waste your resources, — that is, your money, time or talents, by either using them in the wrong way or by not using them at all. You may be tempted by your appetite for food or power or sex, — all of which can be misused. You may be tempted by things, which are not wrong of themselves but which can divert your time and attention from important values like truth, justice and mercy. You may be tempted to measure values with an "elastic yardstick" like those who recognize no absolutes.

One of the best weapons against temptation is fear. The fear of wrong and its consequences is not cowardice. The all-time best way to deal with temptation is to avoid it. Don't run with people who will tempt you. Run from temptation. Don't go to places where there are temptations. Spend your life with people who share your values, and you will reduce your risks. Another weapon is self-discipline. That includes self-control, which itself avoids the need for outside control. Self-control is a character trait which must be nurtured and developed so as to become strong enough to successfully deal with temptations by adherence to moral and ethical values.

Young people are at special risk. A misguided spirit of "adventure" leads some to succumb to the temptations associated with drinking and dope. The mistaken notion of invulnerability, along with the loss of self-control to peer pressure, leads some to simply give away, albeit temporarily, the difference between themselves and the animals, — their brains.

But let me give you some reassurance. The Bible says:

> There hath no temptation taken you but such as is common to man: but God is faithful, who will not suffer you to be tempted above that ye are able; but will with the temptation also make a way to escape, that ye may be able to bear it.[285]

Now don't consider that reassurance to be a license to test temptation. Take the way of escape; and don't play with fire. Fire burns. Be smart. Avoid the consequences of wrong by fleeing temptation. Be true to your values. That defines integrity and produces self-respect.

Self-respect is not self-centered. Indeed, there is a great difference between the two. First, self-respect does not show the arrogance or smugness of self-centeredness. Self-centered people are of all the most miserable, because they can never get as much attention from others as they crave and others never cater to them as much as they fancy they deserve. They want more, and feel they get less, of everything they seek. They get more, and feel they deserve less, of ev-

---

[285] I Cor. 10: 13.

erything they despise. Over and over in this book, you will
see that you should grow out of self-centeredness and into
self-respect.

Self-confidence is born of achievement. If you try to do
something and succeed, that is achievement and it gives you
self-confidence. You know that you can perform that task,
whatever it may be. This leads you to try other things, some
even more difficult. Each time you succeed, your self-confidence increases and your willingness to try new and different challenges is enhanced. This expands your potential,
and frees you to make greater use of your talents and resources.

Set goals for yourself. Your goals should be realistic.
They should be difficult, but not impossible. Try hard to meet
your goals, and you will most often succeed. Then if at first
you don't succeed, try again. You must try; and you must
use what Dr. Norman Vincent Peale called "the power of
positive thinking". Winston Churchill once made a very short
speech to a group of young people. He simply said: "Never,
never, never, never give up!" Fear of failure is self-fulfilling
prophesy; it leads to failure. Success breeds success. When you
achieve, you gain self-confidence; and with self-confidence you
can then set even higher goals and reach them, too.

Self-confidence is a basis for independence; but self-esteem is dependent on others and their approval or disapproval — whether fair and proper, or not. Either of the two
can become "self-centered," which is another matter entirely.
Self-centeredness is the badge of immaturity. We have already talked about that.

Now, if you have self-respect and self-confidence your
bearing and behavior will be enhanced. Your poise and com-
posure will give you a sense of dignity, and others will ob-
serve it. The dignity which comes of self-respect and self-
confidence is perceptible. Others will sense that dignity. It
will affect their attitude toward you. You will be treated with

respect, and you will have earned it. On the other hand, if you have no respect for yourself, you can hardly expect others to respect you. So earn the respect of yourself and others by your own integrity and achievement.

In real life, all of us have failed to reach this high standard. At some time or place — and perhaps at many times and places — each of us has done wrong. As is said in the Scriptures,

> For all have sinned, and come short of the glory of God; . . .[286]

So there is reason for each of us to feel guilty.

Not long ago I saw a bumper sticker which expresses the sentiments of a sizable number of people. It said, "Screw Guilt!" Sadly for those who adhere to that point of view, guilt cannot be so lightly dismissed. Indeed, if it be not dealt with in a proper fashion, guilt will utterly destroy peace of mind.

Generally speaking, a person may deal with guilt in one or two of three ways. The first is more diagnostic than therapeutic, in that one must first decide whether there is a realistic reason for guilty feelings. This is not an invitation to rationalize misbehavior. It is an effort to measure behavior by realistic standards, and to not just wallow in guilt at the behest of legalistic perfectionism. Any realistic person soon learns that choices are not always to be made between what is plainly right and what is plainly wrong. All too often one must choose between what is better and what is best; or between what is painful and what is worse; or between one's own welfare and that of another. Such choices do not call for disregard of moral and ethical standards but,

---

[286] Rom. 3: 23; and see I John 1: 8, 10.

instead, their appropriate application in sometimes uncontrollable circumstances. There are some absolutes; but more often choice of behavior is kin to its context.

The second method of dealing with guilt is apparently embraced by enough of the people in America to make it appear to be the norm. It's example is the bumper sticker which says, "Screw Guilt!" Its methodology is to replace moral and ethical values with an "anything goes" philosophy. If "anything goes" there is no occasion for guilt. This philosophy is seldom directly expressed. On the contrary, it is usually disguised in euphemisms. Evil is redefined and given a new name which sounds palatable. For example, the issue may be framed in terms of "freedom." If freedom of choice be itself right, then may not one make whatever choice suits one's purpose? Use of a laudable term "freedom" implies that *any* choice is acceptable; and the euphemism becomes destructive of societal standards. Morals and ethics cannot be so lightly dismissed. "Freedom" of choice, properly understood, presupposes choice between different but equally moral alternatives, between different but equally ethical patterns of behavior.

There is a third way of coping with guilt. It is in seeking and embracing forgiveness. The Christian gospel message is that, in the redemptive death of Jesus Christ, God offers forgiveness to all men.[287] This is the essence of Christianity. But God's forgiveness was not introduced by the Christian gospel. Nehemiah wrote:

But Thou art a God of forgiveness, gracious and compassionate, slow to anger, and abounding in lovingkindness;

And Thou didst not forsake them,[288]

---

[287] Luke 24: 44-48; I Cor. 15: 1-17; I John 1: 7; Eph. 4: 32.
[288] Speaking of the children of Israel in the wilderness.

Even when they made for themselves a calf of molten metal . . .[289]

So did the Psalmist sing of God's redeeming love.[290] It was preached by the prophets Ezekiel[291] and Isaiah, the latter of whom recounted his vision and the Lord's words as follows:

> Wash yourselves, make yourselves clean;
> Remove the evil of your deeds from My sight.
> Cease to do evil,
> Learn to do good;
> Seek justice,
> Reprove the ruthless;
> Defend the orphan,
> Plead for the widow.
> Come now, and let us reason together,
> Says the Lord,
> Though your sins are as scarlet,
> They will be as white as snow;
> Though they are red like crimson,
> They will be like wool.[292]

Not unlike Christianity, Islam appears to focus on the forgiveness of "believers." Yet the Quràn speaks of forgiveness out of the mercy of Allah.

> And whoever does evil or acts unjustly to his soul, then asks forgiveness of Allah, he shall find Allah Forgiving, Merciful.[293]

---

[289] Neh. 9: 17-18. (NAS)
[290] Pss. 51; 130; 31: 5; 32: 5; 86: 5. (NAS)
[291] Ezek. 19: 21-22; 33: 14-16. (NAS)
[292] Isa. 1: 16-18 (NAS)
[293] *The Quràn*, Surah IV: 110.

God's forgiveness is complete, and carries with it the expiation of guilt. This must be accepted about God's forgiveness: it is not by our merit or worth that He forgives us. It is by His grace, His lovingkindness, His mercy. So don't think there is a way in which you must earn God's forgiveness, or that you are too bad to be forgiven. His grace is sufficient. Moreover, as God forgives, then one must learn to likewise be forgiving of oneself and others.[294] Indeed, forgiveness of others may well be a condition to our own forgiveness. The Lord's Prayer says as much, and Matthew quotes Jesus as having said:

> For if you forgive men for their transgressions, your heavenly Father will also forgive you. But if you do not forgive men, then your Father will not forgive your transgressions.[295]

This forgiveness of others benefits us even more than the others, who sometimes are not even aware of our grudges against them. But the grudges cause tension, bitterness and sour stomachs to those who bear them; and such negative feelings can be avoided by forgiveness.

Forgiveness sets us free, — not to more misbehavior but from the intolerable burden of guilt. Its condition is repentance,[296] which means a turning away from that which caused the guilt. Isaiah put it bluntly: "Cease to do evil, learn to do good."[297] With repentance, there is no more occasion for guilt. Forgiveness works.

Everybody wants to be loved. Everybody wants to be popular. Too often we measure our self-worth by our popu-

---

[294] Matt. 6: 14-15; Mark 11: 25-26; Luke 17: 3-4.
[295] Matt. 6: 14-15. See also Mark 11: 25-26.
[296] Luke 13: 1-5; Acts 2: 37-39.
[297] Isa. 1: 16-17. (NAS)

larity, and that's a terrible mistake. Popularity is almost the same thing as peer approval. It relates to the number of friends you have and whether those friends seem to like you. The real question is whether your friends like you for the right reasons. In large measure, that depends upon your values and the values of the crowd. Often the most popular person is the best "jock." But he is not necessarily the best person. In some groups, taking drugs is the behavioral norm. "Straight" people are not popular in those groups.

This leads us to what we call "peer pressure." It can be either good or bad, depending upon the values or standards of the group. Friends can and do exert peer pressure. If the friends have high standards, they will be supportive of each other in doing what is right and proper. On the other hand, if one is drawn to a crowd which engages in antisocial behavior, their peer pressure will be difficult to resist and trouble will be the result.

In any event, your self-worth should not depend upon popularity but on your own adherence to high standards of morals and ethics. Remember again what Shakespeare wrote:

This above all: to thine own self be true,
And it must follow, as the night the day,
Thou canst not then be false to any man.[298]

One of the problems teenagers have is teasing by classmates, who will play on others' insecurities in efforts to deal with their own. For example, those who don't do well in school, maybe because they are not as intelligent as others or maybe because of their own laziness, often belittle classmates who try to do well. They call them "nerds" or "dorks" or some other such name, whatever is the slang of the times.

---

[298] Shakespeare, *Hamlet*, Act I, Scene 3, line 75.

By teasing — or even insulting — students who do better, they try to bring everyone else down to the level of their own lack of achievement.

But to be embarrassed by achievement is just plain foolish. In the real grown-up world, the achievers do better in every way. Achievers must never let the underachievers drag them down to the latter's level. Those who do make their own future far more difficult, in college and in life. Schooling is not an end in itself; but the means to prepare for one's future as an adult.

Don't compare yourself to others. Don't let others compare you to others. Measure yourself only against the yardstick of your own potential. All of us are different, and none can be fairly compared to another. All of us have potential in the talents given to us by God. The measure of a person is whether his own talents and skills are developed and used to a good purpose in a fashion consistent with the highest standards of moral conduct and ethical behavior. Like it or not, you must measure yourself against that yardstick.

Whether other people succeed or fail is of no concern as you examine yourself. Know that you will make mistakes, and be prepared to learn from them. But never find an excuse for your failures by comparing yourself to others. Likewise, never take too much pride in your own achievements because they are nothing more than to be expected, given your talents.

Remember now, measure yourself by integrity and achievement. The yardstick for the latter is your own potential. Nothing less.

Afterword

The same God who created the seas, the stars, and the "cattle on a thousand hills" gave you life. Don't dare to think it was without a purpose.

You have a free will. You can decide whether to think yourself a victim of chance and circumstances or to take control of your destiny. The choice is yours. And if you take control, you can decide whether your life will be wasted in self-centeredness or used in the purpose for which your Creator daily sustains your spirit. The choice is yours.

You yourself bear responsibility for the person whom you will become, because that person will be formed in large measure by your own choices. Those choices should be purposefully consistent with a system of values soundly grounded in religious, philosophical and cultural principles. You have seen some of those principles and their sources in the preceding chapters of this book and, hopefully, you now realize that the internalization of these values will have a positive and lasting effect upon your choices and the person whom you will become.

Life is not easy. Like all of the rest of us, you will make mistakes. Mistakes are not excuses to quit. Even after mistakes, other days will come and other choices will confront you. If you have detoured, turn back to the right way. Your heredity and your environment will no doubt influence your choices and your life, but they are not excuses for failure to reach your own potential.

Your life has a purpose in God's system of things. Identify your talents and take advantage of your opportunities. Develop your self-respect through integrity and your self-confidence by effort.

You can do these things; and, if you do, you will become the person whom you would like to be.

The choices are yours!

Glossary

Note: There are broader definitions for most of the words listed here; but here are shown the meanings of the words as used in this book.

Aberrant — Not normal.

Abet — Assist or aid.

Absolutes — Principles which cannot be controverted, even in part.

Abstinence — Keeping oneself from something forbidden.

Abstraction — Mental impression or idea.

Academia or Academe — The culture of education, particularly higher education.

Acceded — Gave in.

Acquiescence — Passive agreement.

Acquisitive — Seeking possession or control.

Advocate — One who speaks for another.

Affirmative Action — Advantage given because of race or gender, usually by or at the instance of government.

Alms-giving — Charity.

Atheist — One who denies the existence of God.

Antithesis — Opposite.

Apocrypha — Biblical writings accepted as scriptural by some churches but not by others.

Assimilation — Joining another culture.

Autocrat — Ruler.

Baccalaureate — First full college degree.

Baffled — Without understanding.

Barony — Territory ruled by a nobleman.

Beatitudes — Conditions of blessedness.

"Beg the Question" — Argue backward from the conclusion already held.

Belligerence — Threatening attitude.

Canon — Church law.

Caste — Social group.

Civility — Tolerance and courtesy.

Collegiality — Shared respect and authority or stature among members of a group.

Confidant — Person in whom one confides.

Conjugal — Having to do with marriage.

Consequences — The results of an action or effort.

Context — Related surroundings or circumstances.

Continuum — Measure which increases or decreases by degree from beginning to end.

Correlative — Matching or related.

Corruption — Bad or unlawful behavior.

Credibility — Believability.

Cynic — One who distrusts others.

Deconstructionists — Those who oppose accepted principles.

Deferential — Politely accommodating.

Despotism — Dictatorship.

Diagnostic — Evidence of a disease.

Dignity — Visible self-respect.

Dissidents — Objectors.

Diversity — Differences.

Doctoral — Advanced college degree.

Dole — Government welfare payment.

Ecclesiastical — Related to Church or religion.

Elite — Of higher standing.

Enclaves — Neighborhoods.

Equilibrium — In balance.

Et Cetera — And so forth.

Ethics — Standards of behavior for a profession or business.

Euphemism — A word or expression which makes an idea sound better than it truly is.

Exorcism — Casting out of devils.

Expiation — Wipe out by atonement.

Exploitation — Using for one's own purposes.

Genuflect — Bending the knee before an altar or priest.

Ghettos — Neighborhoods occupied by only one race or nationality, such as where Jews were required to live in some European cities.

Gilded — Covered with a thin layer of gold or made to shine.

Grace — Unmerited favor.

Hedonism — Aimed at physical pleasures.

Hypocrites — Those who say one thing and do another.

Hypothesis — Idea or assumption not proven.

Hypothetical — Unproven supposition.

Iconoclastic — Destructive of sacred objects or traditional principles.

Imperative — Absolute or authoritative.

Impunity — Without punishment.

Inculcate — Teach.

Indictment — Charge of crime or wrongdoing.

Inextricably — Without possibility of separation.

Inhibit — Restrain.

Injunctive — Ordered, as by a court.

Inquisitorial — Asking questions, usually accusatory.

Integrity — Wholeness of character or virtue.

Intellectual — Having to do with mental processes.

Intellectualism — Belief that the only merit is in learning and intellectual activity.

Internalize — To make a part of one's thought processes or basic assumptions.

Intuitively — Without conscious thought.

Inundated — Flooded.

Invulnerability — Having a defense which cannot be overcome.

Jargon — Language used by a profession or trade.

Laudable — Praiseworthy.

Legalistic — Conforming to the letter of the law.

Libertarianism — Belief that one may do whatever pleases him.

Literacy — Ability to read and write.

Manifest — Plainly seen or understood.

Matriarchal — Headed by females.

Matriculated — Entered into a higher level of school.

Melded — Combined or blended into a whole.

Menial — Requiring little skill.

Meritocracy — Advancement and position based on demonstrated ability.

Millennium — One thousand years.

Minutiae — Small or inconsequential details.

Miscreant — Wrongdoer.

Monogamous — Having only one spouse.

Monopoly — Economic interests under the control of a single person or firm.

Monotheism — Belief that there is only one God.

Nexus — That which connects people, things or ideas to each other.

Norm — The usual or typical.

Obtuse — Dull.

Ostensibly — Seemingly.

Oxymoron — An expression that appears to contradict itself.

Palatable — Enjoyable or acceptable.

Pander — Appeal to baser instincts.

Paradigm — Perfect example.

Paradox — A conclusion which appears to be contrary to its premises.

Paranoid — Unreasonably fearful.

Peer pressure — Influence of associates.

Pejorative — Demeaning.

Perceptible — Evident to one or more of the senses.

Perennial — Recurring.

Perfectionism — Compulsive effort to avoid error or mistake.

Perforce — Necessarily.

Pernicious — Bad or harmful.

Perplexed — Without understanding.

Pervasive — Running throughout.

Pharisaical — Practices of the Pharisees.

Pilfer — Steal.

Pique — Annoyance.

Postulate — Claim or argue for.

Potential — That which can be accomplished, realized or gained.

Predicate — First requirement of an act or argument.

Premise — Basis or grounds of a conclusion.

Prerequisite — Condition or requirement.

Pretentiously — With show of courtesy or deference.

Promiscuity — Disloyalty to one's spouse or sweetheart.

Propagation — Distribution or spread.

Protege — Beneficiary of an older influential person.

Proximity — Closeness.

Puberty — Hormonal changes related to early stages of maturing.

Racism — Negative attitude toward others because of their race alone.

Rationale — Reason or explanation.

Realistic — Provable by evidence or argument.

Redemptive — Payment given to recover something from restraint or possession by another.

Relevant — Related.

Repentance — Change of belief and behavior.

Replicate — Reproduce.

Reprehensible — Bad.

Rote — Memory without understanding.

Secular — Other than religious.

Servitude — Slavery to another.

Simplistic — Thought which does not consider the complexities of an idea.

Skeptic — Doubter.

Slough — Pass off.

Solicitous — Concerned about and looking out for.

Spectrum — Range.

Speculation — Guesswork.

Statistical Analysis — Use of numbers to draw conclusions.

Subsidies — Government assistance payments.

Superficial — Touching only the surface.

Syllogism — Conclusion reached by deduction, assuming that attributes of a group are shared by all its members.

Synch — Working together.

Tangential — At the edge or periphery.

Temporal — Limited by time.

Tenets — Principles.

Tenured — With job security, permanent or for a term.

Theoreticians — Those who accept unproven ideas.

Therapeutic — Curative of disease.

Titillates — Appeals to desires.

Trivia — With little meaning or significance.

Truncated — Cut off.

Unmitigated — Without reduction or lessening.

Utopia — Perfect country or community.

Values — Worthwhile standards of behavior.

Variables — Differences.

Vice — Immoral conduct.

Victimization — Avoidance of responsibility by blaming others.

Vilified — Spoken about in a mean or harsh way.

Vivified — Infused with life.

Zakat — "Alms-tax" or charity required by the Quràn.

Bibliography

ABA News (September 1974).

The American Heritage Dictionary, 2nd College Edition (Boston: Houghton Mifflin Co., 1991).

Aristotle, *On Man In The Universe*, Classics Club, ed. by Louise Ropes Loomis (Roslyn, N. Y.: Walter J. Black, Inc., 1943) *Nichomachean Ethics*.

Robert Bellah, et al., *Habits of the Heart: Individualism and Commitment in American Life* (1985).

William J. Bennett, *The Book of Virtues* (New York: Simon & Schuster, 1993).

William J. Bennett, *The De-valuing of America* (New York: Simon & Schuster, Touchstone, 1994).

Allan Bloom, *The Closing of the American Mind* (New York: Simon & Schuster, 1987).

Catherine Drinker Bowen, *The Lion and the Throne* (New York: Little, Brown and Company, 1956).

Donna Britt, Washington Post Writers Group, *Lexington (Ky.) Herald-Leader,* Dec. 5, 1994.

Norman F. Cantor, *The Civilization of the Middle Ages* (New York: HarperCollins Publishers, Harper Perennial, 1993).

Stephen L. Carter, *The Culture of Disbelief* (New York: Doubleday-Anchor Books, 1994)

Stuart Chase, *Tyranny of Words* (Harcourt Brace, 1959).

Cicero, *De Legibus* (as quoted in Benjamin Fletcher Wright, Jr., *American Interpretations of Natural Law* (New York: Russell and Russell, Inc., 1962).

John Dominic Crossan, *Jesus, A Revolutionary Biography* (San Francisco: Harper, 1994).

Reginald G. Damerell, *Education's Smoking Gun* (New York: Freundlich Books, 1985).

James L. Dennis, "For the Common Good", *Trial* (September 1990).

Peter Drucker, *The New Realities* (New York: Harper & Row, 1989).

Peter Drucker, *Post-capitalist Society* (New York: HarperCollins Publishers, Harper Business, 1993).

Michael Fogler, "Lexington Can Escape the Competitive Prison"', *Lexington (Ky.) Herald-Leader,* July 9, 1995.

Milton Friedman, *There's No Such Thing as a Free Lunch* (Chicago: Open Court Publishing Co., 1975).

Milton and Rose Friedman, *Free to Choose* (Harcourt Brace Jovanovich, 1980).

William Alva Gifford, *The Story of the Faith* (New York: The MacMillan Company, 1946).

Newt Gingrich, *To Renew America* (New York: HarperCollins, 1995).

Bob Glauber, The Sporting News, *Lexington (Ky.) Herald-Leader,* Nov. 20, 1994.

Mireille Hadas-Level, *Flavius Josephus, Eyewitness to Rome's First-Century Conquest of Judea,* Translation by Richard Miller, (New York: Macmillan Publishing Company, 1993).

F. E. Halliday, *England, a Concise History* (London: Thames and Hudson, Rev. Ed., 1989).

E. D. Hirsch, Jr., *Cultural Literacy: What Every American Needs to Know* (Boston: Houghton Mifflin Co., 1987).

Oliver Wendell Holmes, Jr., *The Common Law* (Boston: Little, Brown & Co., 1881).

Holy Bible, King James Version.

Holy Bible, Revised Standard Version.

Holy Bible, New American Standard Version.

Philip K. Howard, *The Death of Common Sense* (New York: Random House, 1994).

John Paul II, *Crossing the Threshold of Hope* (New York: Alfred A. Knopf, 1994).

Flavius Josephus, *Antiquities of the Jews,* Translation by William Whiston (Grand Rapids, MI: Kregel Publications, 1901).

Thomas a' Kempis, *Of the Imitation of Christ* (New York: Thomas Nelson & Sons, 1931).

William Kilpatrick, *Why Johnny Can't Tell Right from Wrong* (New York: Simon and Schuster, 1993).

C. S. Lewis, *The Great Divorce* (New York: Macmillan, 1946).

Thomas W. Lippman, *Understanding Islam* (New York: Penguin Group, Mentor, 1990).

Julius J. Marke, *Vignettes of Legal History* (South Hackensack, N.J.: Fred B. Rothman & Co., 1965).

David Martin, "What Makes People Good?" *National Review* (September 9, 1991).

William H. McNeill, *The Rise of the West* (Chicago: The University of Chicago Press, 1991).

Daniel Patrick Moynihan, *Pandaemonium* (Oxford, Oxford University Press, 1993).

John Cardinal O'Connor, Archbishop of New York, quoted in "Who Was Jesus?" *Life Magazine,* December, 1994.

P. J. O'Rourke, *Parliament of Whores* (New York: Morgan Entrekin, The Atlantic Monthly Press, 1991).

J. B. Phillips, *When God Was Man* (New York: Abingdon Press, 1955).

Terry Pluto, Knight-Ridder News Service, *Lexington (Ky.) Herald-Leader,* Dec. 5, 1994.

Paul Prather, "Churches Must Face Issues . . . Head-on", *Lexington (Ky.) Herald-Leader,* October 1, 1994.

The Quràn (Elmhurst, N.Y.: Tahrike Tarsile Quràn, Inc., Translation by M. H. Shakir, 8th U.S. Ed., 1993) .

William Raspberry, Washington Post Writers Group, *Lexington (Ky.) Herald-Leader,* May 3, 1994.

William Raspberry, Washington Post Writers Group, *Lexington (Ky.) Herald-Leader,* Nov. 18, 1994.

J. M. Roberts, *History of the World* (London: Penguin Books, 1990).

Arthur M. Schlesinger, Jr., *The Disuniting of America* (New York: W. W. Norton & Co., 1992).

Hans Selye, *The Stress of Life,* rev. ed., (New York: McGraw-Hill Book Co., 1978).

Shakespeare, *Hamlet* .

C. P. Snow, *The Two Cultures* (Cambridge: Cambridge University Press, Canto Ed., 1993).

Lloyd Paul Stryker, *For the Defense* (Garden City, N.Y.: Doubleday & Company, 1947).

Tacitus, *Annals XV,* xxxiii-xliv, as quoted in Gifford, ibid.

William M. Taylor, *Moses, the Law-Giver* (Grand Rapids, MI, Baker Book House, 1961 reprint).

Alvin and Heidi Toffler, *Creating a New Civilization* (Atlanta: Turner Publishing, Inc., 1994)

The Torah (Second Edition of the translation by The Jewish Publication Society of America, Philadelphia, 1967) .

U. S. Bureau of the Census, *Statistical Abstract of the United States: 1995* .

U. S. Bureau of the Census, *Statistical Abstract of the United States: 1996* .

Ravi Zacharias, *Can Man Live Without God* (Dallas: Word Publishing, 1994).

Suggested Reading

— FICTION —

Fantasy
(Stories of the Supernatural)

The Lion, the Witch and the Wardrobe: A Story for Children, C. S. Lewis. (The first of *The Chronicles of Narnia.*)

The Screwtape Letters, C. S. Lewis. (Adult reading in how tempters come to people, as told in morally inverted letters from a senior devil to his nephew, an apprentice named Wormwood.)

This Present Darkness, Frank Peretti. (The forces of good battle the forces of evil, which try to take over a small college town.)

Romantic
(Adventures of Heroes)

Robinson Crusoe, Daniel Defoe. (How to survive with what can be found in nature, when shipwrecked on an uninhabited island.)

Beau Geste, Percival Christopher Wren. (A young Englishman tells of his service in the French Foreign Legion.)

The Greatest Salesman in the World, Og Mandino. (A motivational story, replete with worthwhile values.)

Historic
(Stories set in a Real Time and Place, Usually in the Past)

The Greatest Story Ever Told, Fulton Oursler. (A dramatized account of the life of Jesus.)

Les Miserables, Victor Hugo. (The French Revolution.)

The Adventures of Tom Sawyer, Mark Twain. (Boyhood in the 1800's in a small town on the Mississippi River.)

The Secret Garden, Frances H. Burnett. (A classic story of young people whose lives are changed when they meet each other and cultivate a secret garden.)

Christy, Catherine Marshall. (An early 20th century story of a young girl who becomes a schoolteacher in the Great Smoky Mountains.)

— NONFICTION —

Religion

Mere Christianity, C. S. Lewis. (Lewis presents "a layman's view" of the essentials of Christianity without arguing doctrinal or denominational differences.)

Orthodoxy, G. K. Chesterton. (An autobiographical Christian apologetic by an English writer with a sense of humor.)

More than a Carpenter, Josh McDowell. (An easy-to-read common sense answer to the question: "Was Jesus Lord, liar or lunatic?")

New Testament Christianity, J. B. Phillips. (A translator of the New Testament shares his insight into "this new quality of living".)

The Twelve, Edgar J. Goodspeed. (The story of Christ's apostles, from both the Biblical account and other records.)

A Shattered Visage: The Real Face of Atheism, Ravi Zacharias. (A modern apologetic.)

Philosophy and Ethics

Nicomachean Ethics, Aristotle. (Early Greek thought.)

De Legibus, Cicero. (Roman philosophy.)

The Book of Virtues, William J. Bennett. (A compendium of cultural, ethical and societal values, together with their sources and stories by which they have been transmitted from one generation to another.)

The Closing of the American Mind, Allan Bloom. (A professor tells how higher education in America has deserted values for the sake of "openness" in lifestyles and ideologies.)

The Culture of Disbelief, Stephen L. Carter. (How American law and politics have come to trivialize religious devotion.)

Secular

Cultural Literacy: What Every American Needs to Know, E. D. Hirsch, Jr. (An encyclopedia of facts and beliefs common to American culture, which writers and speakers take for granted and which their readers and listeners need to know in order to understand them.)

Democracy in America, Alexis deTocqueville. (The classic study by a foreigner of the politics and culture of America in the 1830's with observations as valid now as then.)

A History of Knowledge, Charles Van Doren. (An easily readable story of when, how and what mankind has come to know, from prehistoric days until the present; with the author's forecast of the 21st century.)

Pandaemonium, Daniel Patrick Moynihan. (Ethnicity in international politics.)

The Disuniting of America, Arthur M. Schlesinger, Jr. (The risk to America in the hyphenation of its citizenry.)

Biography

For the Defense, Lloyd Paul Stryker. (A biography of Thomas Erskine — 1750-1823 — whose "battlefields were the courts of justice of Great Britain".)

Abraham Lincoln, Carl Sandburg. (A comprehensive biography by an author who devoted a lifetime to the study of Lincoln — 1809-1865 — and his times.)

Yankee From Olympus, Catherine Drinker Bowen. (The life of Oliver Wendell Holmes, Jr. — 1841-1935 — author of *The Common Law* and Associate Justice of the Supreme Court of the United States, a giant in the development of American law.)

Clarence Darrow, Irving Stone. (A splendid biography of Darrow — 1857-1938 — who was the epitome of a lawyer for the working man whose battles he fought during the late 19th and early 20th centuries.)

About the Author

Robert J. Turley

Robert J. Turley was born in Mt. Sterling, Kentucky, where he lived before moving to Lexington to attend the University of Kentucky College of Law. He has been a trial lawyer for almost 50 years. In addition to serving on committees of several bar associations, he served as Chairman of the Federal Judicial Selection Commission of Kentucky for four years. He is a Diplomate of the National Board of Trial Advocacy and a Fellow of the American College of Trial Lawyers. He is listed in *Who's Who in American Law*, as well as in *The Best Lawyers in America*.

For many years he has been active in the Shriners, especially with their hospitals for children. He has served as General Counsel of Shriners Hospitals for Children and since 1981 as either an elected or emeritus member of its Board of Trustees, which is responsible for the operation of the 22-unit system of hospitals. Over the years, they have rendered free care to more than a half-million children.

Among the awards of which he is very proud are the Trinity Baptist Church Civic Appreciation Award and the Henry T. Duncan Memorial Award given to him by the Fayette County Bar Association.

Turley has four children and eight grandchildren. His grandchildren were the inspiration for his book, *The Choices Are Yours*.

Articles by Robert J. Turley

"Revisiting Luke 11:45, 52", *Ky. Bench and Bar*, Vol. 59, No. 1, Winter 1995.

"Where Do We Go From Here?" *The New Age Magazine*, Vol. 45, No. 8, Aug. 1987.

"The 'New' Doctrine of Comparative Negligence in Kentucky", *Ky. Bench and Bar*, Vol. 11, No. 1, Jan. 1985.

"A Realistic Route to Recognition of Specialization in Kentucky", *Ky. Bench and Bar*, Vol. 40, No. 4, Oct. 1976.

"Pretrial Interview With the Physician", *Ky. Law Journal*, Vol. 58, No. 3, 1969-70.

"Woe To You Lawyers", *Ky. State Bar Journal*, Vol. 30, No. 5, Sept. 1966.

Review of Blum and Kalven, "Public Law Perspectives on a Private Law Problem: Auto Compensation Plans", *Ky. Law Journal*, Vol. 55, No. 1, 1966.

"Citizens for Educational Freedom — The Constitutionality of Its Stated Aim", *The New Age Magazine*, Vol. 78, No. 3, March, 1965; reprinted *The American Rationalist*, Vol. 10, No. 9, March, 1966.

"Changing Times", *Masonic Home Journal*, Vol. 80, Nos. 17 and 18, June 1, June 15, 1964.

"A Call to Counter Revolution", *Masonic Home Journal*, Vol. 79, Nos. 4, 5 and 6, Nov. 15, Dec. 1, Dec. 15, 1962; reprinted *The Scottish Rite Torch*, Vol. 30, No. 5, May, 1963.

"The Verdict Is Yours", *Survey*, Vol. 5, No. 136, Feb. 1963.

"Madison Avenue — Pennsylvania Avenue, — and Main Street", *Oleikan*, Vol. 7, No. 9, Sept. 1962; reprinted *Masonic Home Journal*, Vol. 78, No. 23, Sept. 15, 1962.

"Gaidry Motors, Inc. v. Brannon: Dealer's Duty to Inspect Used Cars", *Trial and Tort Trends — 1958 Belli Seminar*, Matthew Bender & Company, 1959.